AMERICA BETRAYED!

Marlin Maddoux

HUNTINGTON HOUSE INC.

TO MARY

FOREWORD

America Betrayed is a timely book written by a well-informed man of God. It truly exposes the subtle inroads of humanism, but does so in a spirit of love and understanding.

Marlin Maddoux is not on a soapbox. He is not trying to establish himself as an authority on humanism. He is simply sharing a burden of his heart. No one can read this book and ever again be silent about the dangers of creeping humanism.

It is the very best on the subject I've ever read. It should make the devil really mad.

DAVID WILKERSON
Author, *The Cross and the Switchblade*

TABLE OF CONTENTS

Page

SHOCKED INTO REALITY

A strikingly attractive lady sat across a table from me in the interview room of a Dallas, Texas radio station where I host a daily talk show called "Point of View."

A few weeks earlier her name had been mentioned to me as a possible guest to discuss what seemed to be a personal crusade she was conducting. She sounded just controversial enough to be a good guest, and I knew that controversy always generates a large listening audience with lively questions and comments on the phones. The subject would make a good show.

So I said, "Let's go with it."

I had launched "Point of View" because I had kept asking, "Why doesn't someone in the communications business give the people who do not agree with a particular viewpoint a forum to speak out?"

After watching the news reports on television for years, I felt that the whole truth was not being given to the American people. And I had listened to various radio "talk shows" and found that the host would usually make people feel foolish if they even suggested that the moral Christian viewpoint was anything but an item from ancient history.

After waiting for someone to give an opportunity for an alternative voice on the issues, I decided that if no one else would do it, I would have to do it myself. And so — "Point of View" radio talk show was born. We adopted the slogan "The talk show that's *different!*"

The program features interviews with a variety of notable personalities from across the nation and from many different professions. Politicians, entertainers, ministers, crusaders, the famous and the not-so-famous have been guests on the show. Sometimes a guest will simply share a testimony or debate a controversial subject. At other times people will appear on the show who have a "cause" or an issue they want to discuss.

And my guest that day had what she considered to be an "issue" of importance that should be brought to the attention of the people.

I had seen several newspaper articles about her and her work and frankly thought to myself, "Why doesn't she stay at home and mind her own business? Why is she so upset at something as trivial as a few bad words in some of the public school textbooks? After all," I reasoned, "the kids have probably seen worse words on the walls of the school restrooms." I thought she was criticizing a system about which she knew very little.

When she arrived at the station about half an hour before air time, I escorted her to the interview room and helped her unload a large bag full of papers, magazines, notebooks and school textbooks, and wondered how she expected us to wade through so much material in only a couple of hours.

After we were seated at the interview table, we chatted about the format of the show. I told her that we would talk together twenty to thirty minutes, and then I would invite the listeners to call in and ask questions. She was quite nervous, she told me, because she had never been on a radio talk show before. I told her just to relax and talk to me and not worry about the people who were listening on radio.

I noticed that she had relaxed as I put on my earphones just in time to hear the familiar downbeat of the theme music and the voice of the announcer saying, "This is 'Point of View' — the talk show that's *different!* And, now here's your host, Marlin Maddoux."

As the theme music faded, the engineer in the control room looked through the glass window and gave me the "cue" that our microphones were "hot."

We were on the air!

I spoke into the microphone. "Hello, everybody. Thank you for joining us today. We're going to be discussing a subject that should be of interest to everyone — school textbooks! Our guest today has some misgivings about the directions that public education is taking and has mounted a campaign to do something about it. She is speaking out locally, as well as on the state level. I think you will find her a very interesting guest."

With that brief introduction I removed my headphones, laid them down on the table, looked at my guest and said, "Tell me why you are so concerned about what is being taught in the public schools."

By this time my guest had completely relaxed, and when she began to talk she sounded as if she had been doing radio talk shows all her life. She was bright, articulate, sensitive, and had all her facts straight.

She said, "Mr. Maddoux, when my son was in the fifth grade I was serving as program chairman for our school's Parent-Teacher Association. I had read an article in the newspaper that described a history book that purportedly devoted three lines to George Washington and six pages to Marilyn Monroe. Now I am a history buff and 'minored' in history in college, and that information disturbed me. If this was true, I started to wonder if that kind of emphasis might be in other textbooks as well."

She continued, "I had heard of a woman who was speaking out on the school textbook issue, so I invited her to speak to our PTA group. To my surprise, a large number of parents came to hear her. Our speaker convinced me that something, indeed, was wrong in the way we were educating our children; and I became very distressed over this new information and spent the next three months crying and reading. Finally, I stopped crying and continued my research, determined to share what I had learned with other parents."

Her story unfolded as she said, "It became quite apparent to me, as well as to many others, that our children's 'values' were being changed from our traditional values of home, family, and church to some educator's view of what the child's values should be. Our country was founded on the Judeo-Christian system of morality, and we had assumed that was what was being taught. I was also shocked that our children were not being taught the principles of the 'free enterprise' system. I found that some of the textbooks speak favorably of the Marxist-Leninist concept of society and economics and severely criticize the free enterprise system, saying that it is responsible for the plight of the poor."

By this time I knew that she had not only my attention but the attention of thousands of other people as well. This lady was accusing our public school system of the worst of crimes — willfully tampering with the loyalties and the religious and moral beliefs of our children — **without the parents' knowledge or consent!**

My mind could not accept it. It was too "far out" to be taken seriously. It couldn't be! She must be one of a large number of "reactionaries" who don't understand the progressive mood of the country.

My guest continued by saying that further investigation confirmed her worst fears. She concluded, after months of research, that the American public school system was being used to systematically alter the moral values of our children, undermine patriotism and love of country, denigrate the free enterprise system, foster dependence upon the federal government, and create a new society based on what she called **secular humanism!**

After having gone nearly an hour into the interview, investigating the textbooks and other materials, I was clearly surprised at the information I was seeing and hearing. And as if to add insult to injury to the shocked talk show host, my guest, Mrs. Jo Ann McAuley, shoved one of her many books in front of me and said, "Mr. Maddoux, would you please read a few pages from this book? This is a book that is available in public school libraries all across the nation."

Without a moment's hesitation I said, "Of course, Mrs. McAuley, I would be happy to."

And I began to read. Out loud! Over the air!

As I was reading into the microphone, my eyes were traveling several words ahead of what I was actually saying over the air — fortunately! And what I saw stunned me. I stopped in mid-sentence and looked up at my guest. She was looking back at me. Smiling!

I said, "Jo Ann, I can't read this. There are laws that prohibit using that kind of filthy language over the air. Why, the Federal Communications Commission could take our license away from us if I read these words into this microphone. We have decency laws."

With the smugness that comes from seeing a well-laid plan work out right, she just continued to smile. Then it dawned on me. That's the way she had planned it! To shock me! I had been set up! She knew I couldn't read that over the air. She knew I would have to stop. She had a point to make and she made it — at my expense! And I played my part well.

She said, "Isn't it interesting, Mr. Maddoux, that the law will not allow you to read these words over the air, but our children can check this book out of the libraries in our public schools and read it any time they please?"

I would have dismissed what she had to say, but she had the facts in front of her, and I read paragraph after paragraph from the public school textbooks she had brought that backed up everything she was saying. The simple fact was that I was being "educated," along with thousands of others who were listening on radio. The mail we received after that show confirmed that people were shocked, outraged, frightened, angered, and that they wanted to hear more on the subject.

AFTERSHOCK

The information to which I had been exposed that day started me on an intense investigation that was to reveal some shocking facts. I approached the subject cautiously because I didn't want to become a "conspiracy" buff, seeing a sinister plot in every event that took place. But there was something happening in our country, and I was determined to find out what it was.

For the next several weeks after the interview with Mrs. McAuley, I spent every spare moment gathering and reading material on the history and development of the modern humanist movement. As the months passed, things began to fall into place in my mind. What was unfolding was not pleasant. I was repulsed by its implications. It was threatening and not a little frightening. But I felt that my search was helping me to "get a handle" on the reasons why our society was going through such turmoil, with old values being torn down and a new system of morality being erected on its ruins.

I was beginning to see why I had begun to feel like a stranger in my own country.

During the next several weeks I haunted book stores and libraries trying to find something that would give me the "key" to this whole story. I found that humanism is very elusive, for it kept changing its name while retaining its enmity to God and moral absolutes. I ran across such names as naturalistic humanism, scientific, ethical, democratic, religious and Marxist humanism. Other philosophies that seem to crowd under the same umbrella are such things as skepticism, deism, rationalism, liberal religion, agnosticism, and free thought. They all claimed to have descended from classical Greece and Rome, the Renaissance, and the so-called "enlightenment," right down to our modern "scientific" world.

One afternoon I returned to my office after having been on the air for two hours, laid my briefcase down, dropped in my chair, put my feet up, and leaned back to "catch my breath." After a few minutes, my wife, Mary, came in, handed me a small book and said, "A listener brought this by. He thought you might find it interesting."

When she handed it to me the name on the cover caught my eye. It read Humanist Manifestos I and II. I knew what a "manifesto" was. And I was beginning to understand what a humanist was. So, I thought this might hold some answers for me.

I turned the book over and read the comments of the publisher, Prometheus Books: "Publication of the Manifesto has provoked worldwide debate over humanist recommendations for the future of mankind in the areas of religion and ethics and over humanist views on the meaning of life, civil liberties and democracy, the right to suicide, abortion and divorce, euthanasia, sexual freedom, worldwide ecological and economic planning, and the building of world community."

What I was about to read was going to jar me into reality. These documents proved that what had been a loosely knit movement operating under a variety of names was now becoming more defined. This was a call for those who rejected the concept of an eternal

God who created the universe to unite and rid mankind of such philosophical baggage. They had the "new religion of man," and their manifestos outlined how it would be implemented throughout the world.

Humanism became an organized "secular religion" with clearly defined doctrines and goals when a group of humanists thrust upon the world these two documents — which articulated their beliefs about mankind, the universe, religion, and moral values as well as serving as their battle plan and guide for bringing about a worldwide society based upon the religion of humanism.

I was holding those documents in my hands.

THE HUMANIST MANIFESTOS

I later did some background reading on the birth of these two documents and discovered that in 1933, thirty-four people drafted the first of these documents, which in their minds was concerned with the "establishment of a religion worthy of the day's scientific and social advances." This was Humanist Manifesto I and it contained fifteen theses, all to the effect that there was no God and nothing higher than man existed in the universe. This document affirmed that all is "secular" and "relative."

Humanist Manifesto I was signed by an interesting blend of prominent people, including some Americans, many of whom appeared in "Who's Who in America." The list includes such people as John Dewey, an educator and father of the American "progressive" education movement; R. Lester Mondale, brother of former Vice President Walter Mondale; Albert Eustace Haydon; and Charles Frances Potter, along with some pastors and influential writers.

Forty years later a second document appeared that restated and updated the original doctrines and goals of the first one. This second document was signed by such people as Paul Blanchard, author; Joseph L. Blau, professor of religion at Columbia University; Bette Chambers, president of the American Humanist Association; Edd Doerr, Americans United for Separation of Church and State; Alan F. Guttmacher, president of Planned Parenthood Federation of America; Mordecai M. Kaplan, rabbi and founder of the Jewish Reconstruction Movement; Corliss Lamont, chairman of the National Emergency Civil Liberties Commission; B.F. Skinner, professor of psychology at Harvard University; Betty Friedan, founder of the National Organization For Women; and many others. Humanist Manifesto II was heralded on the front pages of major newspapers and publications throughout the world when it was published.

These documents were followed by the 1980 Humanist Declaration. This document decried "reappearance of dogmatic authoritarian religions," as evidenced by "fundamentalist, literalist and doctrinaire Christianity." This restatement of the humanist doctrine was signed by sixty-one scholars and writers, mostly American and British, including B.F. Skinner, Isaac Asimov, Sidney Hook, A.J. Ayer, and many others.

After glancing over the long list of important people who had signed these documents, I was eager to see what they had to say. As I read I was totally dumbfounded at the arrogance displayed. It was hard for me to believe. I had the distinct feeling that these people *believed that they have the answers for the future of the human race.*

Here are a few brief excerpts from Humanist Manifestos I and II:

> The next century can be and should be the *humanist* century. Dramatic, scientific, technological and ever-accelerating social and political changes crown our awareness. We have conquered the planet and explored the moon, overcome the natural limits of travel and communication; *we stand at the dawn of a new age,* ready to move farther into space and perhaps inhabit other planets. Using technology, we can control our environment, conquer poverty, markedly reduce disease, extend our life-span, significantly modify our behavior, alter the course of human evolution and cultural development, unlock vast new powers, and provide humankind with unparalleled opportunity for achieving an abundant and meaningful life. Humanism is an ethical process through which we all can move, above and beyond the divisive particulars, heroic personalities, dogmatic creeds, and ritual customs of past religions or their mere negation. We affirm a set of common principles that can serve as a base for united action. *They are a design for the secular society on a planetary scale.*

As I read further I could sense the obvious hostility of the authors to the very concept of God and Christianity. Their disdain is clearly spelled out, leaving no room for doubt. They consider Christianity to be a roadblock to their design for the secular society on a planetary scale." They say:

Today man's larger understanding of the universe, his scientific achievements, and his deeper appreciation of brotherhood, have created a situation which requires *a new statement of the means and purposes of religion.* While this age does owe a vast debt to traditional religions, it is none the less obvious that any religion that can hope to be a synthesizing and dynamic force for today must be shaped for the needs of this age. *To establish such a religion* is a major necessity of the present.

Though we consider the religious forms and ideas of our fathers *no longer adequate,* the quest for the good life is still the central task of mankind.

As in 1933, humanists still believe that traditional theism, especially faith in the prayer-hearing God, assumed to love and care for persons, to hear and understand their prayers, and to be able to do something about them, is an *unproved and outmoded faith.*

It is our conviction that *humanism* offers an alternative that can serve present-day needs and guide mankind toward the future. Traditional moral codes . . . fail to meet the pressing needs of today and tomorrow. False "theologies of hope" and messianic ideologies . . . cannot cope with existing world realities.

We believe . . . that *traditional dogmatic or authoritarian religions* that place *revelation, God, ritual,* or *creed* above human needs and experience do a disservice to the human species.

We find insufficient evidence for the belief in the existence of a supernatural; it is either meaningless or irrelevant to the question of the survival of and fulfillment of the human race. As non-theists, *we begin with humans, not God; nature, not deity.*

Too often traditional faiths encourage dependence rather than independence, obedience rather than affirmation, fear rather than courage. But we can discover *no divine purpose* . . . for the human species. While there is much that we do not know, humans are responsible for what we are or will become. *No deity will save us; we must save ourselves.*

Promises of immortal salvation or fear of eternal damnation are both illusory and harmful. Modern science discredits such historic concepts as the "ghost in the machine" and the "separable soul" (emphasis added).

Not only did they denigrate the Christian faith; they also stated that the Christian moral value system was outdated and would be replaced with their own "humanistic" morality. They even give us an insight to what that *new morality* will be. They state:

Humanity, to survive, requires bold and daring measures. We need to extend the uses of scientific method, not renounce them to fuse *reason* with compassion in order to build *constructive social and moral values.*

We affirm that moral values derive their source
from human experience. *Ethics is autonomous
and situational,* needing no theological or ideological sanction. *Ethics stems from human need
and interest . . .* We strive for the good life *here
and now.*

In the area of sexuality, we believe that *intolerant attitudes,* often cultivated by *orthodox
religions* and puritanical cultures, unduly repress
sexual conduct. While we do not approve of
exploitative, denigrating forms of sexual expression, neither do we wish to prohibit, by law or
social sanction, sexual behavior between consenting adults. The many varieties of sexual exploration should not in themselves be considered
"evil." Short of harming others or compelling
them to do likewise, individuals should be permitted to express their sexual proclivities and
pursue their life-styles as they desire. *Moral
education* for children and adults is an important
way of developing *awareness* and *sexual maturity* (emphasis added).

Whenever I have attempted to use the statements
found in these documents to pin down the basic beliefs
of humanism, I have found that humanists tend to
downplay their significance. They say there is no
single person or organization that speaks for all
humanists and that these documents are only the
private thoughts of a small group of "free thinkers."

However, when you take a closer look at the people
who signed these documents, you cannot discount
their importance. Some of the most influential opin-
ion-molders in the history of this nation were either

signers or affirmed supporters of the doctrines contained in these three documents. And many of these
people are presently occupying some of the loftiest
positions in academia, business, finance, government,
the arts and communications industry.

The Humanist Manifestos essentially established
the name "humanist." It is their term. They defined it
for us. So the person who ascribes to the doctrines
articulated in Humanist Manifestos I and II has been
defined *by them* as a "humanist." I think we can
therefore safely say that humanism is rightly articulated for us in Humanist Manifestos I and II and the
Humanist Declaration of 1980.

The foregoing statements should remove any doubt
as to the designs of the humanist movement. Plainly
stated, they intend to transform society into a humanistic one, with the religion of that new society
being humanism. In fact, one of my guests said that
when he interviewed some of the leaders in the humanist movement, they made no apologies about
their ultimate intentions of bringing about their worldwide goals. To the contrary, they were quite open and
outspoken about their aims and purposes, perceiving
their plans as the only sane and workable approach to
the survival of mankind in this atomic age.

The humanist movement's goals are clearly spelled
out in their documents, Humanist Manifestos I and II.
They are there for everyone to read. It is their "declaration," their "intention," their battle plan, their grand
design for every human being upon the face of the
earth. *And we would be wise to take them very
seriously.*

WHAT IS HUMANISM?

When I first started using the term "humanism" on the radio and during my talks at churches and conferences, a lot of people responded — sometimes quite angrily — saying, "But aren't we all humanists — in that we are all human beings and are interested in the human race?"

Naturally, the meaning of specific words may vary with different societies and may even change with the passing of time. So I think it is important to define our terms.

First, humanism is not to be confused with "humanitarianism" or "humane." A "humanitarian" is a person who promotes human well-being. All Christians are "humanitarians" in that they have a concern for the good of all mankind. And "humane" is simply a quality marked by compassion, sympathy or consideration for others.

Second, a humanist is not to be confused with those who are engaged in the study of the humanities, such as philosophy, literature and the fine arts.

Third, humanism is not a buzzword that is used as a "catch-all" for describing the people who are not sympathetic to the Church, Christianity, or the Bible. It is, in fact, a legitimate term that describes a definite philosophical viewpoint concerning the world and moral values.

Well, then, just what is it? I have found that it has so many faces that it is difficult to define without going through several college courses in philosophy. But here are some definitions that are accepted by many knowledgeable educators with whom I have talked:

"Humanism" is defined by *Webster's New Collegiate Dictionary* as "a doctrine, attitude, or way of life centered on human interests or values; esp: a philosophy that asserts the dignity and worth of man and his capacity for self-realization through reason and that **often rejects supernaturalism**" (emphasis added).

The *Oxford Dictionary* defines "humanism" (fourth definition) thus: "Humanists are a class of thinkers which arose in Germany toward the end of the 18th century, originating chiefly from the writings of Rousseau. Their system, usually called humanism, sought to level all family distinctions, all differences of rank, all nationality, all positive moral obligations, all positive religion and to train all mankind to be men of the highest accomplishment."

Further, I discovered that humanism is a *philosophy and system of thought and action* that teaches that man has the capacity for self-fulfillment and correct ethical conduct **without God**. Its doctrine makes man the center and rests solely on human interests and values. It denies the existence of God — and teaches that man has no soul, there is no eternity, no heaven and no hell. Humanism, in fact, worships the creature rather than the Creator.

The word "humanist" was first brought into popular use during the Renaissance and originally conveyed the idea of concern for humanity. Many prominent philosophers, teachers, and theologians of the 19th century gave impetus to the humanist movement by adding their support, making it popular to be a humanist. Darwin's theory of evolution seemed to add the final blow to theology's credibility by providing a so-called "scientific" basis for the philosophy of the development of man and the universe, thus doing away with the concept of divine creation.

EVOLUTION AND HUMANISM

The doctrine of humanism rests on the foundation of the theory of *evolution*.

Astronomer Carl Sagan, creator, chief writer, and host-director of the public television series "Cosmos," appeared on the cover of the October 1980 issue of *Time* magazine. Mr. Sagan espouses the humanistic view and has an incredible propaganda vehicle — his television program — for influencing millions of people with his beliefs. The article in *Time* says of him, "Sagan also issues some open challenges. To creationists, who argue for a biblical interpretation of life's beginnings, he states that evolution is not theory; it is fact."

To the contrary, Mr. Sagan, evolution is not *fact*; it is not even *scientific*. It is a *philosophy*, a *theory*, a *metaphysical conclusion*, as any knowledgeable scientist will admit. But evolution is crucial to the religion of humanism. If it can be proven that man was not created by God, but simply evolved from lower forms of life, then man is left to create his own system of morality. But if, in fact, man was created by God, then the theories of humanism are destroyed, and man is accountable for his life on earth.

The theory of evolution is probably the biggest hoax ever foisted on intelligent people. Even though it is a widely accepted theory, it is held mostly by those who have already rejected a belief in God. Thomas Huxley, an avowed atheist, admitted that evolution was only a hypothesis. Other scientists have had to acknowledge that there are no "missing links" and no substantial evidence for the theory of evolution. Therefore, we must conclude, that the theory of evolution is based on faith and not upon fact. And since science is the study of fact, **evolution is therefore unscientific.**

Dr. Duane T. Gish, director of the Institute for Creation Research in San Diego, California, says that evolutionists base their belief on an act of faith, just as creationists do, stating, "No scientist has ever observed the origin of life or the evolution of anything. Actually, the fossil record supports creation, not evolution. When they talk about their evolutionary theories on the origin of life, they are operating outside the limits of empirical science. They are in the realm of metaphysics, not science. The fact is that among all those fossils not one intermediate or transitional form demanded by the theory of evolution has been found."

MAN'S NATURE

In any study of humanism, the name of Jean Jacques Rousseau (1712-1778) will always be prominent. He was a French skeptic whose influence on the thinking of college professors and students alike has accounted for much of the continuing spread of humanism from one generation to the next.

As stated earlier, the *Oxford Dictionary* defines humanism as having "originated chiefly from the writings of Rousseau. Their system, usually called humanism, sought to level all family distinctions, all differences of rank, all positive moral obligations, all positive religion . . . " (emphasis added).

Rousseau did not believe that man s problems stemmed from a corrupt nature. Rather, he reasoned that his problems were the result of his environment and forces outside himself. Rousseau put it like this: "If man is good by nature, as I believe to have shown him to be, it follows that he stays like that as long as nothing foreign to him corrupts him."

Historians agree that Rousseau's philosophy was a major factor in bringing about the French Revolution with its atrocities against thousands of innocent people.

Corliss Lamont, an outspoken humanist, reflected Rousseau's rejection of God's revelation of the fallen nature of man when he wrote in his book *The Philosophy of Humanism:* "What the scientific study of human motive shows is that human nature is neither essentially bad nor essentially good, neither essentially selfish nor essentially unselfish, neither essentially warlike nor essentially pacific. There is neither original sin nor original virtue. But human nature is essentially flexible and educable. And the molding or remolding of human motives is something that takes place not only in childhood and youth, but also through adult life."

The great tragedy is that this basic belief (in the essential goodness of human nature) as set forth in the humanist philosophies has influenced to a large extent many of the public institutions in our nation. Even many church denominations have denied the biblical interpretation of the essential fallen, sinful nature of man, espousing instead a "social" gospel that says the problem is not man's nature that must be changed, but man's environment. Thus they cease to preach and proclaim the regenerating power of the gospel and attempt to "regenerate" man through cultural, economic and social programs.

Even though the Bible is quite plain in describing the unregenerate nature of man, many traditional denominations reject it and opt to define their own theology of man. They have a "humanistic" view of man and the world, rather than a Christian view. So-called Christian humanism rejects the traditional concepts of God, prayer, the sacrificial death of Christ, the church, and worship as anachronistic. They teach that ultimate reality is to be found with man and that Christianity is simply a Christ-like dedication to the total well-being of mankind. It is humanism couched in theological terms.

Moreover, the doctrine of humanism is anti-theistic; that is, it denies the existence of God, the inspiration of the Scriptures, the divinity of Christ, the existence of the soul, life after death, and the biblical account of creation. *Humanist Manifesto I* clearly articulates this:

> Religious humanists regard the universe as self-existent and not created.

> Humanism believes that man is a part of nature and that he has emerged as the result of a continuous process.

> Humanism asserts that the nature of the universe depicted by modern science makes unacceptable any supernatural or cosmic guarantees of human values.

Unlike Christianity, which restores man's dignity, humanism robs man of his divine origin and reduces him to being the product of a meaningless accident of nature. Man's dignity is found only in the biblical account which reveals that he was lovingly created by God, not by himself (Psalm 100:3). Man's highest purpose is found in living with and for God, not for himself alone. Man reaches his highest potential in realizing that he was made in God's image (Genesis 1:26), is the finest of God's creations (Genesis 1:31) and views himself as a wondrous and marvelous product of the mind and intent of God (Psalm 139:14). From this perspective man sees that the universe does not revolve around himself, but around God. And God's will and purposes, not man's, are supreme.

Contrast the dignity of being created by a caring and loving God with the doctrine of humanism as expressed in Humanist Manifesto II, under Affirmation Two: "As far as we know, the total personality is a function of the biological organism transacting in a social and cultural context. There is no credible evidence that life survives the death of the body . . ."

A LESSON FROM COMMUNISM

Both communism and humanism have as their foundational doctrine the same rejection of God and the belief that man is the product of evolution. Evolution is vital to both these ideologies. If evolution is disproved, their entire doctrine falls under its own weight.

A study of the advance of communism reveals that after a country has been conquered militarily, it is then subjected to an intense national "indoctrination" in the elements of communism. The communist leaders learned very early that in order to enslave a person, he must be taught to think of himself as an animal with no spiritual purpose and no eternal soul. Once he has been "programmed" to reject God, he is ready to embrace the State as his god and master. The communists know that a person who holds to his belief in God cannot be enslaved. You may imprison his body, but you will never enslave his mind and spirit. Thus the concept of God must be erased from the minds of the people in order for them to be the slaves of the State.

A chilling account of this process of "conditioning" a once-free people is given by Bishop O'Gara in *The Surrender To Secularism.* He was bishop of Yuanling Province in China when the communists took over. He described the mental and moral rape of his people by saying, ". . . when the communist troops overran my diocese they were followed in very short order by the propaganda corps — the civilian branch of the Red forces. The entire population, city and countryside, was immediately organized into distinctive categories — grade school and high school pupils and teachers . . . merchants, artisans, members of the professions, yes, and even the lowly coolies. Everyone, for a week or more, was forced to attend the seminar specified for his or her proper category and there willy-nilly in servile submission listen to the official Communist line.

"Now what, I ask, was the first lesson given to the indoctrinees? One might have supposed that this would have been some pearl of wisdom let drop by Marx, Lenin or Stalin. Such however was not the case. Their first, **the fundamental lesson given was man's descent from the ape — Darwinism!** . . .

"Are you surprised that the Chinese communists

chose Darwinism as the cornerstone upon which to build their new political structure? At first this maneuver amazed me. I had taken for granted that they would begin by expounding the economic principles of Marx. Later on when in a Red jail, the reason for this unanticipated tactic became very obvious to me. Religion must be destroyed. Darwinism negates God, the human soul and the after-life. Into this vacuum Communism enters as the be-all and end-all of the intellectual slavery it has created."

We are aware of the gigantic push by communism to completely take over the countries of Central America. A little item — overlooked by the press — is that when the Marxists assassinated President Somoza of Nicaragua and seized control of that tiny republic, Cuba helped by sending them **one thousand schoolteachers!**

Not soldiers or farmers, but teachers! Why? To teach the children the principles of Marxism. And the first lesson is that **man is the product of evolution — not creation.**

The Bible teaches, however, that God is the Creator of all life, including man and the universe. This does not deny the biological necessity of human involvement, but affirms that life is more than the result of a biological act. The Bible goes beyond the biological and tells us that God is ultimately responsible for each one of us. We are all stamped with the image and likeness of God, making each one of us of great value.

NEW WORLD RELIGION

Secular humanism is a religion!

Naturally, when we think of religion we assume that it requires a belief in God. This is not necessarily so, for religion is any belief a person may have concerning the relationship between himself and the universe. Even if you believe that you are a product of evolution and not created by God, and your conduct reflects that belief, the Supreme Court of the United States has held that is your religion.

In the *Torcaso* vs. *Watkins* case in 1969, the Supreme Court declared that neither the federal government nor any state can "aid those religions based on a belief in the existence of God as against religions founded on different beliefs." The court further specified that "among religions in this country which do not teach what would generally be considered a belief in the existence of God are Buddhism, Taoism, Ethical Culture, Secular Humanism and others."

The famous case that prohibited Bible reading in the public schools was *Abington* vs. *Schempp* in 1963, in which the Supreme Court also held that the "state may not establish a 'religion' of secularism."

It seems logical that since the Supreme Court has declared that secular humanism is a religion, it should be illegal to teach the secular humanistic value system in our public schools. Moreover, any argument that declares that secular humanism is not a religion has been nullified by these Supreme Court decisions.

A COLLISION COURSE

Secular humanism and Christianity are on a collision course. Any system that teaches anything contrary to moral relativism — such as the Christian doctrine of absolute truth and biblical moral standards

— is a threat to the entire humanistic position. And in order for humanism to bring about its desired goals, man must be stripped of his belief in God and moral absolutes. Humanism cannot prevail as long as man believes in God.

The strand of humanism runs through the fabric of many social and political movements bent on establishing a new world order. The most notable of these on the world stage today are Communism and Socialism. Their basic beliefs contain the same enmity toward God and moral absolutes as reflected in humanism.

Nesta Webster stated in *Secret Societies and Subversive Movements:* "The final goal of world-revolution is not socialism or even communism, it is not the destruction of civilization in a material sense: the revolution desired by the leaders is a **moral and spiritual revolution**, an anarchy of ideas by which all standards set up through nineteen centuries shall be reversed, honored traditions trampled and above all, **the Christian ideal obliterated**" (emphasis added).

THE MOSCOW CONNECTION

The stark reality of the human suffering that can be caused by the persecution of a government and society that is hostile to Christianity was brought forcefully to the awareness of thousands of people when Mrs. Freida Lindsay, president of Christ for the Nations Institute, was a guest of "Point of View." She shared the chilling accounts of the plight of two Russian Pentecostal families who were living in a small room in the basement of the U.S. Embassy in Moscow —

afraid to leave, yet unable to emigrate to the United States.

She told us that on June 27, 1978, the Peter and Augustina Vashchenko family, along with Maria and Timothy Chmykholov, pushed past the Russian guards into the U.S. Embassy in Moscow. There were seven of them. They have come to be known as the "Siberian Seven."

Mrs. Lindsay informed us that they had suffered persecution at the hands of the communist government for years. The government had been trying to stamp out the Christian group since the days of the Stalin repression. Members of these two families, as well as others of their group, have suffered reprisals in the form of beatings, loss of their jobs, mysterious deaths, their children taken from them and placed in state orphanages for "re-education," and internment in labor camps; some of them were held in psychiatric hospitals for communist "modification."

She told us further that these families had been trying, since 1963, to emigrate to the United States, but had been unsuccessful. For their "crime" of visiting the U.S. Embassy for visas in the past, they had been sentenced to Soviet labor camps. But in spite of all the persecution, they were determined to try again.

On that fateful day in 1978 when they rushed past the guards to the embassy, they all made it except their 17-year-old son, John. From inside the embassy courtyard they watched as he was caught and thrown to the ground by the Russian guards. Once inside, they knew they could not come out or they would simply "disappear" and would never be heard from again.

They learned later that their son had, in fact, been

beaten nearly to death and had been sent back to their home town.

When we were about an hour into the program, Eldred Thomas, the president of radio station KVTT, suggested that we call the U.S. Embassy in Moscow and ask about the Seven. It was a bold plan, and I liked it.

While "live" on the air, we called the overseas operator and placed a person-to-person call to the U.S. ambassador at the U.S. Embassy in Moscow. We continued the program as the operator worked to get us a line to Russia. After about forty minutes I got a signal that the call was going through. I punched the button on the phone in front of me so that the telephone conversation could be heard over the air. We heard the clicking and whirring and then the ringing of the phone somewhere on the other side of the world.

A man answered, "United States Embassy."

When the operator asked for the ambassador, we were informed that he was unavailable to come to the phone. But I knew the Russian KGB probably had the phone lines "tapped," and I had something to say that I wanted them to hear. So I said to the man who answered, "This is Marlin Maddoux, and we are 'live' on the air from Dallas, Texas. We have just heard the story of the seven Christians who are living in a basement room in the embassy there in Moscow. Thousands of people are listening to us right now and they want to know about their condition and why the Russian government will not allow them to leave Russia. Can you tell us anything about them?"

The man from the embassy was cordial, but answered that there was nothing he could tell us.

But I firmly believe that someone in the Russian government heard that conversation and knows that there are thousands of Christians in the United States who are aware of the plight of these and other fellow believers in their country.

After the program was over, I caught the elevator down to the fourth floor parking garage where my car was parked, got in, and drove away. I was lost in my thoughts, trying to understand the rationale of a government that so feared and hated the Christian message. And I could not understand how Russia, and other communist governments, can do these things to millions of their citizens without an outcry from the civilized world; and why those from whom the voice of moral rage should be coming remain strangely silent.

A few days later while driving to my office, I recalled a newspaper article that talked about the mentality of those who feel justified in stripping millions of their fellow human beings of their fundamental human rights. I hoped I could find it. When I reached my office I searched through several stacks of files of newsletters, articles, magazine clippings, and other printed matter that I had kept just in case I might need them for a future program or for an article in our own "Point of View" monthly newsletter.

Then I found it and stood beside my filing cabinet to read it. It had appeared on the editorial page of the *Dallas Morning News* and was written by Mr. William Murchison, a member of the editorial staff.

Here in a few simple lines was an explanation of the warped reasoning that can lead a person or government to feel justified in oppressing so many of the human race. Mr. Murchison wrote: "It seems to me that religious people mistake themselves in supposing (to the extent they suppose it) that secular humanists are wicked men. Most are exceptionally well-intentioned. Humanists begin — namely, with the eradication of God — communists and fascists end in bloodshed and tyranny. Why not? Each party has reasoned out its own code — a code as good as anyone else's. No — better; so that to enforce it by means of the slave camp is no more than just."

THE NEW WORLD ORDER

When Edith Schaeffer was my guest on "Point of View," I expressed my appreciation for the work she and her husband, Dr. Francis Schaeffer, were doing in educating the American public to the threat of humanism.

A few weeks later my wife Mary and I attended the National Religious Broadcasters convention in Washington, D.C. On the closing night Dr. Francis Schaeffer delivered an address entitled "The Christian Manifesto," in which he pointed out that there has been a fundamental change in the overall way people view the world and life as a whole; that this shift has been away from a world view that was at least vaguely Christian, toward a world view based upon the idea that final reality is "impersonal matter or energy shaped into its present form by impersonal chance."

One of his most enlightening thoughts was his distinction between the "humanist world view" and the "humanist society." He said that the "humanist society" is a group that produced Humanist Manifestos I and II and is made up of a relatively small group of very influential people, including such people as John Dewey, Sir Julian Huxley, Jacques Monod and B. F. Skinner. On the other hand, the "humanist world view," which has thousands of adherents, is the belief in the material-energy, chance concept of reality.

Over four thousand religious broadcasters, representing some of the most influential people in our nation, sat in reflective silence, weighing the implications of Dr. Schaeffer's words. He spoke with the intensity of a man who could be giving his last warning — speaking to people who could help change the course of a nation. And they were being challenged by his words.

We listened as he revealed that those who embrace the "humanist world view" virtually control the general or popular consensus in our society, much of the media, much of what is taught in our public schools, and much of the arbitrary law being produced by various departments of government. He told us the humanists love to use the word "freedom" but that their push for "freedom" — having no Christian consensus to contain it — is the "freedom" that leads to chaos or slavery under the state or under an "elite." Additionally, he said that humanism, with its lack of any final base for values or law, always lead to chaos; and consequently it then leads to some form of authoritarianism to control the chaos that it created in the first place.

He pointed out that even though humanism speaks glowingly of its "concern" for mankind, it, in fact, has no intrinsic reason to be interested in the individual, the human being, and that its natural interest is the two collectives: the *State* and *Society*.

My clear impression, received from Dr. Schaeffer's revelations, is that our nation is being systematically conditioned to accept a totalitarian, humanistic, elite ruling class. The rationale used for the concept of a **one-world, all-powerful** ruling class is that it is the only way to save the world from collapsing economically and socially.

This is the reasoning of the self-anointed social "elite" who feel they are the only ones who have the intelligence and power to prevent mankind from destroying itself. And, if in the process of saving the world they have to destroy the Constitution of the United States and the personal freedom and dignity of the American people, then so be it!

The threat to the Constitution is no fairy tale. It is very real.

INTERdependence

A word that is being used to promote the concept of a one-world government is **INTERdependence**. It is now being used extensively in the media and in school textbooks.

Congressman John M. Ashbrook (R-Ohio) is quoted in the December 1979 *The Fact Finder* as stating that one of the goals of the World Affairs Council, the National Education Association, and the Aspen Institute for Humanistic Studies is to impose upon the United States a *Declaration of INTERdependence*. This would supersede our own Declaration of Independence and the United States Constitution.

In fact, a "Declaration of Interdependence" was signed by 104 congressmen, in 1976, in Independence Hall in Philadelphia. Though it has been virtually ignored by the American people, it is a decided threat to our own U.S. Constitution.

When I read a list of the things for which this new "Declaration of Interdependence" is calling, I had the strange feeling that I had read this rhetoric before. So I got out my copy of Humanist Manifesto I and re-

read Affirmation Twelve. The similarity is not coincidental.

What does this new "Declaration" call for? It calls for the increase of authority of the United Nations, the surrendering of our national resources to all nations of the world, the creation of a new economic order under the regulation of an international supervision, and a world court and world security force.

Incidentally, at the same time that a "Declaration of Interdependence" was called for, a proposal was made for a "World Constitution" in 1987 (the 200th anniversary of our nation's Constitution). This "World Constitution" would eliminate our national identity and reduce the United States to a "region" within a **new global order.**

Again, the public schools will be the propaganda outlet for those advocating the One World doctrine. The schools are being inundated with propaganda promoting the concept of INTERdependence — which emphasizes "global perspectives" and "global citizenship" rather than national pride and United States citizenship.

The Aspen Institute for Humanistic Studies published a report entitled "Coping With Interdependence: A Commission Report." This report says, "In education, it is hardly surprising that school children are not learning to bypass the distinction between the 'domestic' and 'international' when most of their parents are still carrying that too-clear distinction around as intellectual luggage. In looking for a peg on which to hang education for global perspectives, our school systems across the country might do well to use the Declaration of INTERdependence concept which has been creatively put forward as a contribution to the Bicentennial celebration by the World Affairs

Council of Philadelphia."

PROGRAMMING WORLD LEADERS

The Aspen Institute for Humanistic Studies seemed
to regularly appear in the material that I was reading
for my research on the humanist movement. From
what I could read, it seemed to be a highly elitist
organization that was greatly responsible for enlist-
ing, persuading, and indoctrinating some of the world's
most influential people into becoming part of fulfilling
the humanist dream of a one-world government and
society. I was intrigued at the discovery that this
organization attracts people from the top echelons of
the governments of the world, the multi-national corporations, the leading colleges and universities, the
historic church denominations, the major television
and radio networks, the major newspapers and magazines, and powerful financial institutions.

The January 1979 issue of the Freemen Digest
states: "Many people have asked the question:
Where do the leading officials of the Trilateral Commission, the White House, the Ford Foundation, the
Rockefeller Foundation, the Exxon Corporation, the
Brookings Institute, the New York Times, the Ob-
server International, Die Zeit, the IBM Corporation
. . . the Xerox Corporation, the Citibank, the U.S.
University, the World Bank, the Council on Foreign
Relations . . . the Chase Manhattan Bank, etc., go for
advanced seminars in global ideology and humanistic
studies? The not-so-obvious answer is Aspen, Col-
orado. To those who travel in high circles, Aspen is
not just a mountain retreat . . . it is a place where the
world's elite gather to consider the problems of gov-
ernance and to set forth possible plans for the future of

humanity. This organization, which has been one of the world's best-kept secrets, is the Aspen Institute for Humanistic Studies."

Well, after reading this kind of information I decided I should dig a little deeper into the subject. And the best place to go is to the top. So I interviewed the president of the Aspen Institute for Humanistic Studies, Mr. Joseph Slater, by telephone from his office in New York City. Our interview lasted about 45 minutes, and I ran it on "Point of View."

When I asked Mr. Slater to tell me about the Institute, he explained, "Its purposes are to provide seminars for business leaders so that they will be more reflective on questions of values, justice, liberty, freedom, the Judeo-Christian heritage, spiritual and religious issues, issues of the law and the U.S. Constitution. These are people who are in the decision-making capacities in our society."

I asked, "Are you aiming your efforts toward the world leaders?"

"Yes, particularly business leaders," he replied. "But we also have participants from other sectors of society; namely, academic and educational leaders, the media, government and religious leaders, people from the arts and sciences, and all parts of society. In these meetings, leaders exchange ideas on the various issues of the contemporary world — reaching back into history. We're concerned with the deeper issues that have their roots in terms of 'val es'; religious and ethical thought; the Judeo-Christian thought."

I then told Mr. Slater that my research had revealed that a large number of the world's leaders were closely allied with the Aspen Institute; because of this, I felt that it was of concern to many as to what was actually discussed at their seminars because their discussions would eventually affect national thought and could even influence political "happenings" in the United States and the world.

I said, "Mr. Slater, I know of no other organization that has been associated with so many influential people in high places. Can you explain why world leaders find it so attractive?"

Mr. Slater replied, "They need a chance to pause and reflect on the enduring values — what directions and priorities individuals and institutions should set for themselves. And here is a place, because of its independence, where they have a chance to think and communicate with other people who share their concerns. The Institute attempts to reach people who are affecting people's lives. We have found that it has changed a number of people's lives. We have found that it has changed a number of people's lives and viewpoints."

Further investigation revealed that the Aspen Institute for Humanistic Studies has a strange interlocking of board members, trustees, associates, and financial contributors with the same foundations, multi-national corporations, national radio and television networks, government officials, colleges and universities, church denominations, and other various organizations that are active in promoting the humanist dogma. It doesn't seem coincidental to me that these organizations that represent so much wealth and power find themselves financially and philosophically intertwined with the Aspen Institute.

It is frightening to view the scenario that unfolds. Here you have the humanist philosophy of bringing the entire world under one humanistic world government, and an organization dedicated to bringing together the "movers and shakers" of the world community — those people who influence the opinions, philosophies and politics of entire nations.

As I researched this organization and read the list of the people associated with it, I realized that these are the very people who "control" the media and the money in the United States. I cannot believe that these "executive seminars" are as objective and harmless as Mr. Slater would have us believe. Do they want us to believe that international bankers, royalty, leading political figures, billionaire industrialists, prominent scientists, high ranking military men, leading academicians, corporate magnates, newspaper barons and other "elitists" find it profitable to leave their other pursuits to enjoy a simple two week "retreat" where they discuss only the world's great philosophies? Hardly!

ONE–WORLD GOVERNMENT

The Bible teaches that in the end-time there will be a one-world government headed up by one powerful ruler — the Antichrist. This worldwide anti-God movement is propelling the nations toward this end as foretold by the ancient prophets generations ago. If anything would convince me that there must be a God, it would be the present-day fulfillment of Bible prophecy.

The cry for a one-world government is not the raving of a few maniac alarmists. It is the ultimate goal of many throughout the world, including a vast number of people here in America. The plan for a one-world government is clearly spelled out in Humanist Manifesto II, under Affirmation Twelve:

We deplore the division of humankind on na-

tionalistic grounds. We have reached a turning
point in human history where the best option is to
transcend the limits of national sovereignty and
to move toward the building of a *world community* in which all sectors of the human family
can participate. Thus we look to the development of a system of *world law* and *world order*
based upon *transnational federal government*
. . We thus reaffirm a commitment to the building
of a *world community*, at the same time recognizing that this commits us to some hard
choices (emphasis added).

We are told that our "best option" is to "transcend
the limits of national sovereignty." Many of us do not
agree that this is our "best option."
Please read carefully the plans for a "transnational
federal government." This "transnational federal government" would supersede our own Constitution
and Bill of Rights, making us subjects of a "one-
world" government and therefore subject to "international" laws. Many of our nation's politicians,
educators, writers, newsmen, teachers, clergy, and
others espouse this "world community" view. This
philosophy can be seen in decisions in Congress, the
State Department, and the courts, and is vigorously
promoted through the news media and academia.
In 1966, the *Humanist* magazine (July/August)
admitted that their purpose was to *supersede nation-
alistic boundaries* by a world-wide organization that
would possess *international sovereignty* over the
nations of the world. Many in our nation are committed to this aim, even at the expense of the welfare
of their own country.
They propose to move America "beyond nation-

alism" toward this "transnational federal government" in an attempt to merge Western democracies, Eastern communism, and the Third World dictatorships into a single socialist state, bringing about the dream of the philosophers who envisioned three classes of people: the elite ruling class, the ever-present military, and the masses, with no distinction between the sexes. Men and women would work side-by-side and the children would be wards of the State.

ONE–WORLD ECONOMY

In order to bring about one international government, there would have to be a one-world monetary system. This, of course, corresponds to what the Bible predicts in Revelation 13:16-18:

> He required everyone — great and small, rich and poor, slave and free — to be tattooed with a certain mark on the right hand or on the forehead. And no one could get a job or even buy in any store without the permit of that mark, which was either the name of the creature or the code number of his name. Here is a puzzle that calls for careful thought to solve it. Let those who are able, interpret this code: the numerical values of the letters in his name add to 666. (Living Bible)

Unwittingly, I'm sure, the humanists have laid out the plans that, when completed, will serve as the fulfillment of that ancient prophecy. Their plan for this world monetary system is spelled out in Humanist Manifesto II, under Affirmation Fifteen:

The problems of economic growth and development can no longer be resolved by one nation
alone; they are worldwide in scope. It is the
moral obligation of the developed nations to provide — through an international authority that
safeguards human rights — massive technical,
agricultural, medical, and economic assistance,
including birth control techniques, to the developing portions of the globe. World poverty
must cease. Hence extreme disproportions in
wealth, income, and economic growth should be
reduced on a worldwide basis.

Even a cursory reading of this statement reveals
that it calls for universal control of all economies.
This is a system based upon the philosophy of Karl
Marx, not our American free enterprise system. The
humanists are calling for a socialistic, worldwide
economic system with an all-powerful government
(ruling class) that would control all aspects of the
economy. God foretold it generations ago, and man,
in his rebellion, is rushing headlong toward Arma-
geddon.

It is evil for men to plan to destroy the sovereignty
of the nations of the world and merge them into a
totalitarian, humanistic one-world governmental system, for it involves the abolition of all other governments, of private property rights, of inheritance rights,
and of the right to worship God as your heart dictates,
as well as the destruction of national pride and patriotism and of the family as we know it today.

Unless there is a dramatic turn around in this nation, it would not be surprising to see someone appear
on early morning television on all three networks to
make the following announcement: "My fellow Amer-

icans, in light of the imminent danger to this nation and to the world — of economic collapse, the starvation of millions, and nuclear holocaust — the office of president of the United States and the members of Congress have been replaced by a central committee of political and military experts who are better prepared to guide this nation through this crisis. We also want to inform you that the Constitution and the Bill of Rights have been 'temporarily' suspended, and all radio and television stations, all newspapers and the telephone systems have been 'nationalized' for the 'protection' of the public. As soon as the crisis is over we will return to our democratic system of government.

"But until then, please cooperate with your central committee. And, now, here is a member of the committee with instructions for you to follow during this crisis time in our nation."

It *could* happen in America.

2

TAKEOVER OF THE PUBLIC SCHOOLS

Unpleasant realities are difficult to accept graciously. And when I immerse myself in a study that traced the philosophical change that has been imposed on our public school system, I reacted with disbelief and then anger. A series of guests appeared on "Point of View," each bringing enlightenment on yet another aspect to the pervasive influence of secular humanism on our schools and universities.

I had to admit that the humanists' most ingenious move was the systematic takeover of the public school system in America. It showed a special insight, marked by originality, cleverness, and clearness of purpose, and was the most important step toward turning an entire nation away from its original goals to the new goals set forth by organized humanism as articulated in Humanist Manifestos I and II.

As I thought about it, I could see the genius in the

takeover of the system that educates the children. The humanists knew that if they wanted to take over a nation it would have to be through the very young, for when a person has been taught that he is a free citizen in a free country, with the power to make his own decisions, it is impossible to make him adopt the "collectivist" mentality. So they knew they would have to reach for the young, and the place to do that was the public schools. They would begin with the training of the teachers themselves.

While most parents view the public school as the place for our children to receive the education and skills necessary to enable them to lead a useful and productive life, the humanist sees it as something quite different. The humanist educator considers the public school to be an institution of indoctrination.

An article entitled "A Religion for a New Age," published in *The Humanist* (January/February, 1983, p. 26) states:

". . . the battle for humankind's future must be waged and won in the *public school classroom* by teachers who correctly perceive their role as the *proselytizers* of a *new faith*; a *religion* of humanity that recognizes and respects the spark of what theologians call divinity in every human being. These teachers must embody the same selfless dedication as the most rabid fundamentalist preachers, for they will be *ministers* of another sort, *utilizing a classroom instead of a pulpit to convey humanist values* in whatever subject they teach, regardless of the educational level . . . The classroom must and will become an *arena of conflict between the old and the new — the rotting corpse of Christianity, together with all its adjacent evils and misery, and the new faith of humanism,* resplendent in its promise of a world in which the never-realized

Christian ideal 'love thy neighbor' will finally be achieved" (emphasis added).

Charles Frances Potter wrote, "Education is thus a most powerful ally of humanism, and every American school is a school of humanism. What can a theistic Sunday school's meeting, for an hour once a week and teaching only a fraction of the children, do to stem the tide of the five-day program of humanistic teaching?" (*Humanism: A Religion,* 1930).

Mr. Potter would be pleased to know that the teaching of humanism has been systematically integrated into the courses being taught in the public schools of this nation, including everything from history to the life sciences.

JOHN DEWEY

John Dewey was the driving force for humanism in public education in the 20th century. Dewey's influence on public education was enormous. He was the leader of the "progressive education movement" in America, and his theories became their bible.

John Dewey was an avowed atheist and a board member of the American Humanist Association when it created Humanist Manifesto I, and was one of its signers. He rejected all fixed moral laws and eternal truths and principles. He insisted that truth was relative, that absolutes were not admissible, that the evolutionary theory was valid and affirmed, and that there was no God and man did not have a soul.

According to Dewey, man is a biological organism completely molded by his environment; and that environment is constantly changing, as is man. The logical conclusion to the whole matter was that it was useless to teach children any of the moral absolutes, as found in the Scriptures, and the teaching of ethics was a "waste of time."

When Mel and Norma Gabler appeared on "Point of View," they gave me a copy of their book *Textbooks on Trial*. On pages 201 and 202, they say: "Dewey assigned to the schools a revolutionary mission to reform society, including its economic system. The chief instrument to accomplish this reform of our country was the use of social studies instead of the separate disciplines of history, geography, economics, etc. Having changed the aim of the schools . . . new textbooks were written and old ones revised to present the collectivist aim . . . There was emphasis on life-adjustment of the student, learning by doing called the discovery method . . . It was a permissive approach . . . "

The book then charges that the child subjected to the new social studies was being "sensitized." This involves three steps: (1)"unfreezing his values and standards"; (2)"changing the child by giving him different standards and a different conception of who he is"; and (3) "refreezing, to lock the child into the self." The new social studies "has the express purpose of unfreezing the child's home-taught values at an early age."

Mrs. Jo Ann McAuley, who has been a frequent guest on "Point of View," is president of National Congress on Excellence in Education, and is a former member of an eight-member review group convened by the Science and Technology Committee of the U.S. House of Representatives to evaluate the controversial behavioral social science program, "Man: A Course of Study" (MACOS). Her minority report is contained in "Report Prepared for the Committee on Science and Technology, U. S. House of Representatives, Ninety Fourth Congress."

She was asked by the General Accounting Office, the investigative arm of Congress, to participate in a study to assess the use of values-changing curricula in American schools, and by the National Institute of Education, a division of HEW, to assist in a study to determine the problems, issues, and solutions to education in America.

I am indebted to her for sending me the following information under the title "Values-Clarifying or Values-Changing." She states: "Any credible appraisal of the educational dilemma in this country must deal with the obvious failure of the schools to teach our children those academic skills which are needed by them to lead useful lives in our competitive society. Every study of academic performance conducted during the last fifteen years has arrived at the same conclusion — the reading and math skills of our nation's students are *steadily declining*. For twenty years schools have abandoned vital basic skills training to become simply one more institution engaged in social problem-solving."

The paper gave me further insight into the reasons for the deplorable state of our public education system. Under the heading "Progressive Education vs. Traditional (Basic) Education," she writes: "Prior history of schools will show that education dealt with two 'domains.' (1) The *cognitive* domain dealt with the intellect (the act of knowing; perception; awareness); (2) the *psychomotor* domain addressed the need for vocational skills (of or designating muscular activity directly related to mental processes). During this time period, parents were not beating down the school doors.

"In the '20s, John Dewey introduced his 'progressive' theory that children cannot be taught by instilling facts in their brain, but rather, they must 'experience' or 'feel' all things. This practice of dealing with the *feelings, attitudes, values,* and *beliefs* of school children is known as the *affective domain,* and it is here, in this sensitive area, that the schools find themselves in conflict with parents for the first time in their history."

She then laid out some very simple comparisons between these two opposing approaches to education that helped me to understand the sharp disagreement between educators and parents concerning the reasons for the mounting problems in education today. She clearly pointed out the contrasting differences between the "progressive education" of John Dewey, which gained its impetus in the '60s, and "traditional (basic) education" which prevailed up until that time. Here is how she listed the comparisons:

PROGRESSIVE EDUCATION	TRADITIONAL (BASIC) EDUCATION
Reduces role of individual and stresses "collectivism" or "groups."	Stresses individualism as the end product of education.
Believes that memorization is boring and a waste of time. Only "relevant" matters of today are important and nothing in the history of our country, etc., is of consequence.	Stresses facts relative to history, the arts, etc., as a necessary part of learning.
Holds that the pupil should progress at his own speed and compete only with his own best efforts.	Believes that competition is good and necessary for the very survival of our country and that success of the individual in later life depends on his ability to hold his own in a highly competitive world.

Feels that curriculum must adjust to interest and needs of the "group."	Feels that the pupil should attempt to adjust to a curriculum which will provide the individual with the skills and ability to cope in a cultured, productive manner in a democratic society.
Stresses no absolutes (i.e. students make pertinent decisions without authority or standards; responses to questions are acceptable as long as the students can justify or rationalize their replies).	Teaches that there are absolute standards and values, and that the purpose of education is to identify these lasting values and to explore them to benefit the individual and our nation.
Stresses stimulation of the senses and emotions — neglects intellect (i.e., attempts to alter behavior or control emotions).	Stresses education of intellect and believes that emotions and senses develop with the intellectual and physical growth of the individual.

In an article entitled "Three Cheers for our Secular State," Paul Blanchard (a signer of the Humanist Manifesto), wrote, "I think that the most important factor moving us toward a secular society has been the educational factor. Our schools may not teach Johnny how to read properly, but the fact that Johnny is in school until he is 16 tends to lead toward the elimination of religious superstition. The average American child now acquires a high school education, and this militates against Adam and Eve and all other myths of alleged history" (*Humanist Magazine*, March/April, 1976).

In researching the various means used to gain control of the educational system in the United States, I discovered that long ago the humanists infiltrated and gained control of the National Education Association.

The book *The Siecus Circle* says of the NEA: "Recognizing this organization's potential for exerting tremendous pressure and influence on American

education, the Humanist-Socialist complex wasted
no time in seizing control of the NEA; this is accom-
plished as far back as the early 1900s. Early NEA
leaders who strove for a one-world Humanistic order
included such Humanist-Communist fronters as John
Dewey and William Heard Kilpatrick. Harold Rugg
and Marxist professor George S. Counts (who now
serves on the National Advisory Council of the
American Civil Liberties Union) were among the
NEA teacher-leaders whose writings helped steer the
leftward course of this organization in the early
1930s.

"These and other Humanist-Socialist oriented educators spear-headed a master plan to socialize
America under the leadership of John Dewey, then
honorary president of NEA. Humanist Dewey considered NEA to be a potential channel for the dis-
semination of his educational philosophy, which was
based on a wholly materialistic view of life. Through
its official organs and recommended texts, NEA soon
was affecting the methods and thinking of thousands
of professional educators."

BRAINWASH TECHNIQUES

Changing the moral consensus of an entire nation is
a formidable task. As I read about the various methods and techniques employed to alter the moral con-
sciousness of the schoolchildren, I could see why I
and millions of other parents had not recognized them.
The mind-manipulators had couched their techniques
in lofty-sounding academic jargon, devised to bypass
all but those who were privy to their private language.

One of the most important aspects of any method
designed to change the moral value system of the child

would have to appear to be improving the child's ability to "think for himself." If your child's teacher sent home a memorandum which stated in bold letters, **"We are going to rob your child of his Christian values and instill a humanist value system in him,"** you would have protested.

The fact of the matter is that they are doing it. They just do not tell you about it.

The Russian scientist Pavlov developed a technique in which he could condition dogs to respond to him on cue. Human behavioral psychologists have borrowed his methods, using them to condition the human mind. By skillfully employing these techniques, an educator can gradually alter your child's values, behavior, conscience and personality.

These techniques are being used today, beginning in kindergarten and continuing through higher education. They fall under such headings as *values clarification, behavior modification, psychotherapy, group therapy, role playing* and *inquiry.*

VALUES CLARIFICATION

The method known as "values clarification" purportedly helps the student answer such questions as "Who are you? Where are you going? What do you really believe in?" The educators claim not to instill a particular set of "values" into the mind of the child, but only to help him to "clarify" his own values. However, the program is clearly based upon the assumption that there are no absolute values and that all values are "relative, personal, and situational."

One teacher's guide tells the teacher that the child comes to school with his mind in a state of "confusion" as to values; and since the parents and the church have contributed to that confusion, the school must help the student "clarify" his own values. However, upon examining the values actually encouraged, you find them to be godless, immoral, humanistic, without absolutes and entirely unrelated to those of his parents.

"Values clarification" is a method used extensively in our public schools. This method is designed to convince the child that he has the "right" to develop his own personal values and morality — free from authority of any kind, including that of his parents and church. It is designed to instill within the child the belief that there is nothing particularly right or wrong, but that everything is "situational."

Here is the seven-step valuing process which forms the basis of the book *Values Clarification* by Simon, Howe, and Kirschenbaum:

(1) Choose the Value Freely
[This means free from church-dictated concepts of morality and parental influences.]

(2) Choose from Alternatives
[The Judeo-Christian ethic is an ABSOLUTE. It cannot be changed. It was given by God. Here, however, the child is taught to break away from these "restrictive" moral codes and choose his own.]

(3) Choose after Considering the Consequences
[If there is no accountability to God, then you can "do your own thing" with impunity.]

(4) Prize and Cherish the Value
[The child has now become a "law unto him-

self," so the value is his — not God's or his parents.]

(5) Publicly Confess or Affirm the Value
[The Christian knows the power of "confession" of his belief. It reinforces it. Affirming something sinks the value further into the child's subconscious mind.]

(6) Act on the Value
[If you have decided that premarital sex or homosexuality, for example, is all right, then act upon that decision.]

(7) Act upon the Value Regularly
[The child has now chosen a new "life-style." His values are no longer the same as those of his parents, and he intends to live by his own new value system — not by that of his parents or church.]

(Note: The comments are mine.)

Sidney Simon's method of "values clarification" is widely used in elementary and secondary schools throughout the nation. He calls traditional religious and moral training "useless" and says that it is irrelevant today because the modern world is uniquely difficult and complex and that young people are confused. He asserts that the belief that there are "right" and "wrong" ways of acting and thinking is harmful to a child's development and a new approach must be adopted. And, of course, he has the answer — *values clarification.*

Simon's values clarification method suggests that

teachers should indoctrinate the children by asking such "open-ended" questions as: Would you favor a law that would limit the size of families to two children? Would you choose to die and go to heaven if it meant sitting around on a cloud and playing a harp all day? Do you think parents should teach their children to masturbate? What would you rather do on Sunday morning — sleep late, play with a friend or watch TV? Do you approve of premarital sex for boys? For girls? Do you think sex education should include techniques for lovemaking and contraception? Would you like to have different parents? Should we legalize abortion? Do you think we should legalize marijuana? Should homosexuals be allowed to teach in public schools? Do you approve of a couple trying out marriage for six months before getting married? Should we legalize mercy killings?

His values clarification "strategies," he claims, enable the child to achieve knowledge about values **free from the inhibitory inculcation of adults.**

The values clarification principle is based on moral relativism and is designed to change the moral concepts of the student. When this is skillfully presented to a student, it has a profound effect upon his conscious and subconscious mind as well as his moral character and personality.

The humanists want the children to have maximum self-choice in choosing their own values; and to accomplish this they must first break the value system the children bring to kindergarten and first grade which was put there by their parents, church, and society.

After the student has his values "clarified," he will then govern his life-style by a set of moral values at odds with those of his Christian parents. The moral

revolution in this nation is clear evidence to the effectiveness of values clarification in our schools.

ROLE PLAYING

Another method used to bring about behavioral
change is called "role playing." Through this method
the child is placed in the situation of having to make
very deep moral judgements. In one such game several children are in a boat at sea. The boat cannot
hold all of the people in it, so the judgement must be
made to put someone overboard to die. Then various
occupations are listed, and the child must decide
which one is the least important to society and must be
put overboard so that the others may live. The value of
life and death is based purely on the "situation" at the
moment and not upon any absolute laws of God. I
have talked personally to parents whose children were
subjected to role playing games, and they say that
their children suffered much mental anguish as the
result.

The National Education Association defined "role
playing" as sensitivity training (*Today's Education*,
Jan. 1969, pp. 67-68). When role playing, the student
is assuming the role of behavior normally different
from his own and is taught to identify with that particular type of behavior being enacted.

Dr. J.L. Moreno developed role playing for use on
catatonic patients in psychiatric wards. **It is a medical tool for the mentally ill.** The patient must
assume the role wholly and totally and is then subjected to psychological probing in his new identity.
This technique was designed to be used by trained
therapists; but it is being used by teachers in the

classroom, and the potential for disaster is enormous. Though the teacher may be sincere and unaware of the dangers, she should be warned that there is the possibility that the child may assume a certain role and be unable to come out of the role upon leaving the classroom.

Through these brutal scientific behavioral modification games, the child is coerced into revealing his very heart, mind, soul, and subconscious feelings before his teachers and classmates. His values are questioned, forcing the child to defend his value system and show how he arrived at it. Most adults cannot do this effectively. Can we expect a child to do it? Naturally, any value that is derived from parents or church influence is not accepted as having been the freely chosen value of the child himself. So he must replace the "old" values with those he has arrived at himself, free from the influence of anyone else. He has now had his "values clarified."

INQUIRY METHOD

The "inquiry method" is also aimed at "values clarification." Dr. Collin Cooper asked how this method can help anyone find truth and principle, when, as he says, "The principle underlying the technique denies the person any standard by which to judge truth or falsehood." The answer, of course, is that the child is to be convinced that there are no standards other than those he "chooses" freely to follow.

This method is also part of the mind-manipulative and values-changing methods which teach the students to question everything. He is taught "value change" — change in himself, in his community, and in his family. He is also to submit to group consensus, which is pure peer pressure to conform. The child is taught to question authority, reject morality, reform society by external change, and accept man as just another animal.

A teacher is sometimes referred to as a "change agent"; and if she is skilled in her craft she can manipulate the child away from his Christian teaching and create another "convert" to humanism, bringing their dream of a humanistic utopia a step closer to reality.

These brainwashing techniques are devastating the minds of children. If it is not stopped in time, your child will be "reconstituted" so that he will recognize no ultimate authority for morality except himself and his peers. These techniques cause the child to view his parents as ignorant, unloving relics of the past and a threat to his future happiness. Profound alienation between the child and his parents will result.

Most of us would be shocked at the plans some of our "social planners" have in store for future programs for our schools and our children. The book *The Siecus Circle* states: "Hawaii is also the first state to have adopted the revolutionary 'master plan' for education, titled 'Forecast for the '70s,' which appeared in the NEA journal, *Today's Education*, in January 1969. Several major points in this forecast were: (1) Educators will assume responsibility for children when they reach the age of two. Enforced or mandatory foster homes are to be available for children whose homes are felt to have a malignant influence. (2) Children will be given drugs on an experimental basis, to 'improve in the learner such qualities as personality, concentration, and memory.' (3) There will be widespread busing of children to achieve various goals. (4)

Teachers will become 'learning clinicians.' This title is intended to convey the idea that schools are becoming clinics whose purpose is to provide individualized psychosocial treatment for the student . . ."

TEXTBOOK PROPAGANDA

As I dug further into what's happening in education, I discovered that if anyone spoke out and even 'suggested' that there might possibly be some school textbooks that shouldn't be used in the public schools, they were immediately branded as rank *fanatics* who were against boys and girls gaining "knowledge." The word used to discredit these "toublemakers" is "censorship." Many journalist and educators made it sound like these concerned parents were violating the First Amendment rights of every school child in America.

It's simple. If you have material that you want to get to the students and you know the parents — with their traditional moral hang-ups — will object, then you intimidate or shame them into remaining silent. And when some parents do speak up, you ridicule them as being archaic fanatics who fear knowledge. It is just such tactics that have kept parents silent for years.

But, when someone does speak up after having spent the time and effort to plow through hundreds of school textbooks and lay out concisely and intelligently the actual instances where the child is being taught a humanistic value system, then even the press and the publishers have to take them seriously.

That's exactly how Mel and Norma Gabler have become so well known in the executive offices of America's leading publishers of school textbooks. They do their homework.

During one of their appearances on "Point of View," they told me, "For a number of years the educational establishment has been molding the minds of students toward their philosophy but doing it so subtly that the general public has not realized what is happening. Yes censorship is involved — deeply involved. What was done suddenly through government force by Hitler has been done gradually in the United States. Government force, through schools, has gradually eliminated (banned, censored) practically all books that uphold, promote, or teach the basic values upon which our nation was founded. The 'censors' should be asked why there is such a dearth of textbooks and public school library books that support the following: Monogamous families, anti-homosexuality, anti-abortion, American patriotism, morality, conservative views, teaching of honesty, obeying laws, changing bad laws through a legal process, etc. Librarians and curriculum directors call their censorship or book banning *the right of selection.*"

They also gave example after example of the type of material to which they and thousands of other Christian parents object. Among the materials they gave to me was an article they had written entitled "Humanism in Textbooks: Secular Religion in the Classroom," which contains enough material to persuade any intellectually honest person that an attempt to inculcate a new value system into the students is an on-going process. Here are some excerpts from the article, under various categories, that should help you decide for yourself.

EVOLUTION (*As found in public school textbooks*):
".. infants can grasp an object such as a finger,

so strongly that they can be lifted into the air. We suspect this reflex is left over from an earlier state in human evolution, when babies had to cling to their ape-like mothers' coats while mothers were climbing or searching for food" (*Understanding Psychology,* Random House, 1980).

"Many scientists believe that the apparent relationships are because simple organisms gradually developed into more complex organisms" *(Exploring Living Things,* Laidlaw, 1977, Grade 7, Life Science).

SITUATION ETHICS *(As found in public school textbooks):*
"In a society where values are constantly shifting, the young adult may often be confused by which set of values he or she is to follow . . . "
(Toward Sexual Maturity, TRM, Steck-Vaughn, 1980, Grades 9-10 Health).

"Stress that whether specific action is right or wrong depends on the meaning that a given group attaches to the action" *(Around Our World,* TE, Houghton-Mifflin, 1980).

"Some years ago the rules for right and wrong seemed clear-cut and easier to understand. 'Do this, but don't do that.' Today there is a trend to relax such strict standards . . . "(*ME; Understanding Myself and Others,* Bennett, 1982, Grades 6-8 Homemaking).

"There are exceptions in almost all moral laws, depending on the situation. What is wrong in one instance may be right in another. Most children learn that it's wrong to lie. But later they may learn that it's tactless, if not actually wrong, not to lie under certain circumstances" (*Inquiries in Sociology*, Allyn, 1972, HS Psychology).

ANTI–CHRISTIAN (*As found in public school textbooks*):
"Among all the hundreds of Middle Eastern gods, a very different kind of god emerged. This was the God of the Hebrews. Here is a Hebrew children's story that tries to explain how people began believing in this new kind of God . . . " (*People and Culture*, Economy Co., 1982, Grade 6 Social Studies).

One writer has said: "the early Hebrews created the Bible out of their lives; their descendants created their lives out of the Bible" (*Exploring our World — Eastern Hemisphere*, Pollert, 1982, Grade 6 Social Studies).

"Anthropologists studying human customs, religious practices, ritualism, and the priest-craft came to the conclusion that men created their own religious beliefs so that the beliefs answered their special needs . . . The God of the Judeo-Christian tradition was a god worshipped by a desert folk . . . and heaven was high above the desert, cool and pleasant. The Eskimos . . . reversed the concept" (*Perspectives in U.S. History*, Field Educational Publications, 1972, High School U.S. History).

SEXUAL PERMISSIVENESS (*As found in*

public school textbooks):
"Adolescent petting is an important opportunity to learn about sexual responses and to gratify sexual and emotional desires without a more serious commitment" (*Life and Health*, Random House, 1980, Grades 9-10 Health).

"Delbert and Sally are living together while they are in college. They do not expect to marry ... they feel that living together provides each with love, affection, and support" (*Person to Person*, Benact, 1981, Grades 6-8 Homemaking).

"Contrary to past belief, masturbation is completely harmless, and in fact can be quite useful in training oneself to respond sexually ..." (*Life and Health*, Random House, 1960, Grades 9-10 Health).

COLLECTIVISM (*As found in public school textbooks*):
"Some people believe that the federal government should act as the parent of the family — the nation. All problems are to be solved by the national government" (*Exploring American Citizenship*, Glove, 1983, Grade 8 Civics).

"One of the corner stones of most socialist philosophies is ... the freeing of human beings from the burdens of unnecessary and onerous labor in service of profit-makers" (*Sociology: Study of Human Interaction*. Random House, 1976, High School Sociology).

"... TO DISCUSS: Some people feel that the

government should pay every family in the United
States a minimum amount every year if they do
not earn that amount by working. Would you
support such an idea? If so, how much should this
amount be? If no, why not?" (*Government and
Citizenship,* Allyn, 1983).

"The Communist governments provide many
benefits for their workers . . . The governments
also provide for health care, long vacations, and
old-age incomes. Personal incomes tend to be
low . . . but expenses are also low. Most older
people in eastern Europe can meet their daily
needs without much difficulty" (*World Geography,* Follett, 1980, High School Geography).

WORLD GOVERNMENT (*As found in public school textbooks):*
*"To make international cooperation really work,
some people think that the countries of the world
must come together under a world government.
They feel that only with a world government is
there a chance of saving the earth for humankind" (American Citizenship: the Way We
Govern,* Addison-Wesley, 1979, High School
Civics and Government).

"We now live in an age in which we must recognize that our interdependence extends beyond national boundaries, from the local to the
global community" (*Introduction, United States
Government: The People Decide,* Science Research Association 1979, High School Civics).

"Many people think a stronger U.N. or a new

international organization is needed if we and the other peoples of the world are to move safely into the 21st century. Only a stronger world body, they argue, can meet tomorrow's challenges" (*American Citizenship Program,* Scholastic 1977, High School Civics).

"THE FUTURE OF GLOBAL POLITICAL SYSTEMS — You have seen how politics, economies, and the search for justice are all woven together in the fabric of global political systems. Because of increased interdependency, some people predict one increasingly integrated system for global politics" (*American Government: Comparing Political Experiences,* Prentice-Hall, 1979, High School Civics).

As a parent, grandparent or concerned citizen, you must not allow the school to remold your child's mind with secular humanism. You should examine your child's textbooks for any mention of values clarification or any bias against the family and Christian morality. You should have the responsibility (and right) to teach your child to recognize the doctrine of humanism and to watch for the various techniques of "values clarification" being used. Your child should also be advised that he has the right to refuse to participate in any role-playing games involving mercy-killing or suicide or in discussing his innermost beliefs.

One of the most important pieces of legislation to come out of Washington is the Hatch Amendment (Public Law 95-561). It became law on November 1, 1978 and is one of the greatest victories ever won to protect the rights of parents and students in relation to public school policies. The requirements of this amendment have been incorporated into the Education Division General Adminstration Regulations (EDGAR). These regulations govern state and local agencies that receive funds from the Education Department.

This amendment is so important that we print it in its entirety.

PROTECTION OF PUPIL RIGHTS

"Sec. 1250. Section 439 of the General Education Provisions Act (relating to protection of pupil rights) is amended by inserting a new subsection as follows:

"(b) No student shall be required, as part of any applicable program, to submit to psychological examination, testing, or treatment, in which the primary purpose is to reveal information concerning:

"(1) political affiliations;

"(2) mental and psychological problems potentially embarrassing to the student or his family;

"(3) sex behavior and attitudes;

"(4) illegal, anti-social, self-incriminating and demeaning behavior;

"(5) critical appraisals of other individuals with whom respondents have close family relationships;

"(6) legally recognized privileged and analogous relationships, such as those of lawyers, physicians, and ministers; or

"(7) income (other than that required by law to determine eligibility for participation in a program or for receiving financial assistance under such program), without the prior consent of the student (if the student is an adult or emancipated minor), or in case of unemancipated minor, without the prior written consent of the parent."

For years parents have been intimidated by those in public education whose attitude has been "We are the educators, and you, as a parent, are not competent to pass judgement upon our subject matter or methods of teaching your children." However, this attitude is changing, and parents are slowly regaining control over their own children.

3

MEDIA MANIPULATION

A lady told me that her four-year old daughter was sitting in front of the television when the announcer said, "This is the CBS Evening News with Walter Cronkite." The camera zoomed in on the stately, gray-haired Mr. Cronkite, who with a serious expression on his face and a somber tone to his voice said, "Good evening," and then proceeded to report the news.

The little girl, who had grown up accustomed to seeing the familiar face of the grandfatherly newscaster on her television in her home at the same time each evening, turned to her mother and asked, "Mommy, is that God?"

When I heard the story I shuddered to think of the power of television — and other media — on the minds of people, especially the young. Though Mr. Cronkite, I'm sure, would agree that the little girl's mistaken identity of him was an exaggeration, I'm afraid millions of Americans accept the newscasts and the critical analysis of the news by the network reporters with much the same awe and respect that the nation of Israel afforded the thunderous pronouncements coming down from Mount Sinai.

The accusation has been made that some in the medical profession — as well as some of the clergy — develop a "godlike" opinion of themselves as the result of their influence over other people. But the arrogance sometimes displayed by members of these professions cannot compare to that which had developed among the "chosen few" who write, edit, and broadcast the news on the three major television networks. The power that is exerted by these people is far out of proportion to their qualifications or objectivity and has become a real threat to free and diversified thinking in this nation.

So powerful have the three major television networks become that they can bring down administrations, affect the stock market, fan the emotions of the people for or against an issue, or promote a system of morality they favor. The riots, marches, flag-burnings, destruction, disruption and rebellion of the '60s and '70s were prolonged — if not actually created — by the ever-present television cameras and network personnel who were all to willing to be used to promote any radical group that would shout obscenities against the policies of the United States. The very fact that the media was there to cover a story gave it significance far out of proportion to its own intrinsic worth.

The Jane Fondas, the Eldridge Cleavers, the Huey Newtons, the Joan Baezes, the Tom Clarks, and the Abbie Hoffmans could never have gotten their twisted versions of political morality before the American public without the servitude of the cameras and crews of ABC, NBC, and CBS. One radical could draw three network camera crews ready to film his every pronouncement. Month after month after month we saw an endless parade of draft card burnings, sit-ins, fiery speeches from political left-wing radicals — all denouncing the United States and praising Russia, North Vietnam, and Marxism-Leninism.

If the cameras and crews of the networks had withdrawn from these radicals, the movement would have died within weeks. But the protesters had learned to choreograph their demonstrations, giving ample notice to the networks where the action would be, so that they could go to their assignment editors in plenty of time to secure a sizable crew to cover the event. The protesters had learned to "play to the cameras," and the press was all to willing to comply.

No, Susie, the newscaster is not God.

And his report and analysis of the news is not Holy Writ.

THE POWER OF THE PRESS

I am a bonafide, registered, card-carrying member of the working press. The term "press" originally referred to those people who were involved in the print media, paricularly the newspapers. But as other forms of communication developed, the name came to cover all those in any of the various media — i.e., radio and television, as well as the print media.

The press is a person's link to a national audience. Even the president of the United States must depend upon the press to get his message to his constituents. He can speak to only a few thousand people face to face at one time, making it impossible to reach the millions in the nation without having his words transmitted to them via radio, television, or the printed page. So he is at the mercy of the press when it comes to communicating his ideas to the people. This is why wise administrations bring in experts to advise and direct them in their dealings with the national press.

The people of the press *know* that they are the "link" to the people. It gives them a sense of power. Power to make or break. Power to promote or destroy. Power to persuade. Power to intimidate.

I have covered many major events for my radio talk show all across the nation, and I have found that a "press pass" is a magic key that opens almost any door. The sponsors of these events have a "message" they want to get across, and they know the only way to reach a wide audience is through the media. Therefore, the press people are given *carte blanche* to almost any place or person at the event. Guards step back and allow you through when they see your press pass. Usually a special room is set up for you furnished with telephones, typewriters, sandwiches, snacks and drinks, and several people to cater to your slightest desire.

I have "rubbed elbows" at these events with people from NBC, CBS, ABC, *Newsweek, The New York Times,* major religious periodicals, independent radio and television people and a host of other media personalities. It is a heady business. You are recognized by the public, awarded celebrity status, and given special privileges. Famous and powerful people are happy to visit you — usually at your convenience. You are courted, cajoled and pampered, all with the hope that you will give them print space or air time to help them promote themselves, their product, or their cause.

CENSORSHIP IN DALLAS

Let me give you an example of how the news can be censored by a newsperson before it ever reaches your home. In 1980 I was hosting "live" coverage of the National Affairs Briefing for radio station KVTT in Dallas, Texas, where more than twenty thousand people had come to Dallas to hear some of America's most enlightened people discuss the social and moral issues confronting our nation. Our radio equipment was set up on a table not more than fifty feet from the speaker's podium in the Reunion Arena. Immediately behind our table was a platform that supported the television crews and their equipment for the three national networks, and several religious networks, as well as many local television stations.

The man in charge of one of the national network crews sat at our table and visited with us during the breaks. I found that he was totally unfamiliar with the evangelical movement and viewed it with a somewhat suspicious attitude.

When one of the principal speakers at the convention, Mr. Paul Weyrich, referred to the fact that he had at one time been a newspaper reporter, the network man uttered an expletive and muttered, "I can't believe that this guy, who used to be a member of the press, is saying these things."

He then instantly turned around and signaled to his cameraman to "cut" and blurted out, "We don't want that kind of *stuff* going over our network" (only he used stronger language).

I was shocked — to say the least. I tried to think of what the speaker had said that evoked such an emotional response from our network friend. As I reviewed Mr. Weyrich's talk, I remembered that he was simply telling the people how the humanists had gained the upper hand in public education, the news media, and the government, and how the people should and could regain control of these institutions. He was simply exercising his freedom of speech. But it was not the kind of speech that the network man wanted the public to hear — so he refused to let it be seen and heard by the American public.

I have found that it is this kind of "spoon-feeding," in flavors and amounts prescribed by those who control the media, that is the rule rather than the exception.

The stated purpose of the humanist movement is to bring about a one-world, socialistic, anti-God society. And they are moving ahead, for even now a relatively small number of committed humanists profoundly affect the lives, institutions and destinies of over 200 million Americans.

They are able to influence national and world events because they occupy some of the highest positions in the businesses and institutions that influence the information gathering and disseminating agencies.

They virtually control what we read, see and hear.

The influence of secular humanism on the American press is enormous. Most of the nation's leading journalists were educated in the large, liberal "Eastern establishment" colleges and universities and were thoroughly schooled in the religion of humanism. And they bring that mind-set with them when they write the stories that are daily consumed by the American public.

Ask yourself the next time you read the newspaper,

"Who does the editing for this paper? What wire service furnished it? Who were the editors in New York? Who hired the editors and reporters? What are their beliefs? What point of view are they trying to get across?" Any event or story, in the hands of a skilled writer, can be slanted to fit the bias of the reporter by simply applying a slightly negative or positive emphasis to what should be a purely objective item.

It is axiomatic that to control a country you must first control its sources of communication. The television and radio stations and newspapers are among the first targets of any revolutionary movement which attempt to overthrow a government.

When Solidarity became a threat to the communist government in Poland, the government arrested hundreds of the union's leaders, declared martial law, and took over all the communications media — including television, radio, newspapers, and telephones — knowing that one of the requirements for keeping a nation free is the free exchange of ideas and thoughts among the people. When the people are unable to communicate, the government can intimidate them into submission.

It would be folly at this point for any group to attempt to seize the communications media in the United States by force. However, though mental and philosophical seduction of a nation may be slower, it is just as effective and just as deadly.

SAME WORDS — NEW MEANINGS

The dictionary defines "semantics" as "the branch of language study that deals with the meaning of words and their effect on people." Some words have the power to create positive, pleasant feelings while others can induce a negative, unpleasant feeling. A skillful writer can manipulate the emotions of his readers any way he chooses by the use of certain words.

Before I invited Mel and Norma Gabler to appear on "Point of View," I had read an article about them in the November 25, 1979 issue of *Parade Magazine* entitled "Public School Book Censors Try Again." I thought about the article while I was interviewing them, for it was a fascinating study in semantics. I remembered that the article featured a picture of a bonfire, giving rise to memories of Nazi Germany and the massive book burnings ordered by Hitler and his henchmen.

I smiled as I recalled the article, for I knew quite well what the author had in mind when he chose that particular picture. In addition to the skillful use of words, the press can employ pictures to manipulate the mind, inflame the unthinking emotions, distort facts and create the response from the reader that they wish. At first glance I knew that this was not journalism; it was nothing more than a propaganda piece.

Even the headline employed that dread word "censor." Nobody likes a censor. Why, we have a Constitutional amendment guaranteeing freedom of speech and of the press, and we dare anyone to violate it. So with the words and pictures the mood was set. You knew you were about to read the story of some people who were trying to bring back the intellectual suppression the people had felt under Nazi rule.

But I wanted to get the whole story. After such blatant slander, these people should at least have the opportunity to tell their side. I wanted to go beyond the prejudiced writings of the bigoted reporter and get the real facts, because most readers didn't bother to investigate the story any further. They did not stop to ask, "Who are the Gablers? Are they trying to censor what America reads? Do they burn books? Are they trying to do away with our freedom of choice?"

What I discovered was that they do not burn books, nor do they try to censor what America reads. But the writer of the article wanted us to think they did. It was an inflammatory, prejudicial article that reflected the humanistic bias of the writer and served only to distort the real facts. It was not journalism. It was propaganda — pure and simple.

As I began the interview with the Gablers, I tried to visualize these two gracious people tossing little children's school textbooks onto a giant bonfire — and it just didn't fit. As their story unfolded, we learned the truth. They review 'proposed' school textbooks and submit written critiques, in the manner prescribed by the laws of the State of Texas for the Texas School Textbook Committee to read. They are simply exercising one of their rights as citizens of this great nation.

But the humanists are unhappy with the Gablers, for these two individuals are quite effective in pointing out the instances where the public school textbooks undermine the family, the free enterprise system, and the Judeo-Christian moral code. In the process they expose the glut of humanistic indoctrination found in them. And they are being heard! The publishers hold them in high regard. Many don't like them; but they know better than to try to slip a blatant humanist textbook into Texas, for they will meet them head-on.

The interview on "Point of View" showed that the true facts about the Gablers were quite different from what the writer of the article wanted us to believe. Our only conclusion is that he was writing out of his own ideological bias when he labeled their work as "censorship."

MEDIA MONOPOLY

According to the A.C. Neilsen Company, television has a **97 percent saturation** in the United States; and in the average TV household the set is in use **more than 45 hours per week!**

Scientists tell us that we remember 60 percent of what we see and only 10 percent of what we hear. Television and movies combine both sight and sound, hearing and seeing, thereby greatly enhancing their power to persuade. That innocuous "box" that sits in your home may not be as "harmless" as you once thought. You may be getting a lot more than you think when you sit down to watch it.

There are only three major television networks in the whole of America, thereby concentrating this awesome power in the hands of a small circle of "elitists." Others are trying to break this monopoly, but as of this date, ABC, NBC, and CBS remain the principal sources for news and entertainment for the vast majority of Americans.

As bad as television "entertainment" is, it is the news reporting departments of the three major networks that are the most effective in molding public opinion — making them also the most potentially dangerous to a free society. There is no question that these networks have the attention and respect of the American people. Statistics show that we get more of our current events information each day from them than from any other source.

And most of it is slanted toward liberalism!

We have witnessed in this nation the development of a closed "media-society" which advocates a system of values contrary to the traditional Judeo-Christian moral values. The networks are virtually controlled by people who espouse the liberal, humanistic philosophy.

I tried to present this thought to the nation when I was a guest on ABC's "Nightline" in October 1981. I knew beforehand that I would probably not get my questions answered, but I was determined to at least address the issues before a national audience.

I, along with several others, was invited by ABC to ask questions of a panel of ABC news people about the quality of their network's news coverage. The ABC panel consisted of Frank Reynolds, Barbara Walters, Sam Donaldson, and the host Ted Koppel.

During the national telecast I said to Ted Koppel, "I will address my question to you because this subject was alluded to at the beginning of the show. I am a radio talk show host in Dallas and I get feedback from the listening audience that has revealed some very interesting things. Number one, generally speaking, there is a mistrust of the national media. Number two, the press is viewed as a 'controlled' press not controlled by a sinister few, but by what is commonly called the Eastern establishment mentality. And number three, there is a belief that the media have an inbred bias against the traditional moral value system. Could you comment?"

Mr. Koppel answered, "First of all, that we are controlled by anyone, I think, is just wrong. That our bias tends to be Northeastern 'liberal,' I alluded to that, as you quite correctly pointed out. That's one reason why we're here. If that is true, we are trying to make amends for it. To the degree to which we have succeeded, you and all the folks out there who are watching will have to judge."

Mr. Koppel didn't fully recall the third part of my question, so I restated it by saying ". . . there seems to be an inbred bias (in the national press) against the traditional moral value system. . . the Judeo-Christian ethic."

He then replied, "Well, I simply again do not agree with you and I don't know how one goes about proving that with a simple answer. So you will have to accept, for the moment, that I don't think it is true."

THE PROOF EXISTS

To be fair to Mr. Koppel and other sincere journalists, probably very few in the media are consciously aware of their part in carrying out the goals of the humanist dream. They are themselves products of a humanistic educational system, and write and report the news with that inbred bias. They would like for us to believe that there are no hard facts to back up the accusations that I made against the national press on "Nightline." But those facts do exist.

Two scholars, S. Robert Lichter and Stanley Rothman, conducted hour-long interviews with 240 journalists and broadcasters at the most influential media outlets in the country. These included reporters, editors, bureau chiefs and executives responsible for news content. They sought to find out how these journalists felt about controversial issues.

Their findings, published in *Public Opinion* (Oct.-Nov. 1981), revealed that these media elite had voted for the presidential candidate of the Democratic Party by margins ranging from over four-to-one in

1972 and 1976 to fifteen-to-one in the Goldwater-Johnson race in 1964.

While only 54 percent described themselves as "liberal" politically, their votes and their attitudes on a variety of issues suggest that they are overwhelmingly liberal.

This was especially obvious on social questions. Eighty-five percent disagree with the statement that homosexuals should not be allowed to teach in public schools, and 76 percent disagree with the view that homosexuality is wrong. Ninety percent were pro-abortion; 97 percent thought that governments should not pass laws regulating sexual activities. Nearly half, 47 percent, saw nothing wrong with adultery. Eighty-six percent of the media elite said they seldom, if ever, attended religious services, and only half claimed any religious affiliation.

The article continued with some very enlightening information on the philosophy of those who write, edit, and dispense the news in this nation. It clearly reveals that our so-called "free press" is in fact philosophically controlled by secular humanists.

The influence of leftist propaganda on our media elite is evident in the high percentage who indicated that they agreed with such well-known Soviet propaganda lines as the charge that the United States exploits developing countries of the world. Fifty-seven percent took the view that our use of the world's resources is immoral. One out of eight believed that big corporations should be owned by the government. Apparently a significant minority of the media elite subscribes to basic Marxist principles.

Mr. Koppel and others may not recognize it, but the views of the media elite are far more liberal, far more favorable to socialist ideas, than are those of the

general public. However, the fact that they are out of
step with the people does not faze them in the least.
Asked what group ought to exercise the greatest influence in society, they nominated themselves!

YOU'RE GETTING MORE THAN ENTERTAINMENT

Most of us think of television as entertainment.
Would it surprise you if I told you that it is not? And
even though advertisers consider it the greatest selling
tool ever to be invented, its primary function is not
selling goods? No, television is first and foremost an
educational medium. It is an instrument of *persuasion, indoctrination, seduction, propaganda* and
mind manipulation — all done in an entertaining
way.

The most effective methods of persuasion and indoctrination are those that the subject least suspects
of being used for that purpose.

Humor, for example, is one of the best ways to get
past a person's conscious defenses. Then, when these
defenses are down, the "messages" can be sent straight
to the subconscious mind where it will be stored to
eventually affect the thinking and life-style of the
subject.

Picture yourself, along with your wife and children,
having a quiet evening at home. You have worked
hard. You came home, had dinner, got the dishes out
of the way, sat down in your favorite easy chair,
glanced over the evening paper, checked the TV guide,
and flipped on the set. With a drink in your hand and a
bowl of popcorn at your side, you settled in for a
couple of hours of entertainment.

You are now in exactly the frame of mind that the programmer or advertiser had hoped for. When you flipped the "on" button, you welcomed them into your home. They are now your invited guests. But whether you know it or not, your entertainment comes laden with an enormous amount of propaganda, usually reflecting the humanistic value system.

SATIRE AND RIDICULE

The use of satire and ridicule is an extremely effective psychological weapon when skillfully used to avoid any honest discussion of facts.

An example of satire and ridicule being used in television was demonstrated during an episode of "All in the Family." The writer/producer brain trust of the show was able to denigrate marriage, children, motherhood, the family, the Christian minister, the Christian marriage ceremony, and the Christian moral value system, while advocating situational ethics, sex before marriage, non-religious marriage vows, sexual equality and the humanistic value system in marriage — **all within a twenty-nine minute span of time!**

The story line was about a young couple who "Gloria and Mike" had invited to be married in their home. One of the first revelations was that the bride had gotten pregnant while the couple had been living together. The ceremony was principally for the "sake of the bride's mother and father." They had just "slipped up."

When the minister arrived, it was revealed that they had found his name in the Yellow Pages. (No self-respecting humanist would be caught dead knowing a

Christian minister). The Yellow Pages minister, who rode a motorcycle to the wedding, was portrayed as a complete "jerk." His ceremony consisted of a total perversion of the standard Christian marriage cere- mony — which has united millions of couples and laid the foundation for a lifetime of love and commitment to each other. The desecration of the words and spirit of the ceremony was an insult to every husband and wife who have ever pledged their love to each other while repeating its vows.

The only sacred or serious moment in the ludicrous display of blasphemy was when "Mike" read an asi- nine poem about two trees growing side-by-side with- out overshadowing each other. It was a touching scene when everyone got emotional over the poem.

Funny! Everybody is broadminded and has a good laugh. But — the laugh is on *morality, marriage, sex, motherhood* and all those "unenlightened" people who are still *sexually stilted* by *outmoded religious beliefs.*

This is situation ethics being promoted through the situation comedy — over a national TV network!

So much was sent home to the viewer that it is difficult to point out all the areas of anti-Christian, humanistic brainwash. So much was said — *without saying it.*

A humanistic, secularistic value system was taken for granted as being the modern, enlightened way. Christian principles and ceremony were scoffed at and ridiculed. The clergyman was portrayed as mo- ronic, insincere, dull, and totally unnecessary.

Talk about the propagandistic use of satire and ridicule — television writers are masters of it.

MESSAGE, MEDIUM, METHOD

When the writers, programmers, actors, producers, or special money interests have a message they want to send to the American people, they know they have three basic things to consider: the **message**, the **medium**, and the **method**.

The message can be whatever the principals choose to send. The medium may be television, the printed page, radio, the movies, record albums, or any other means of communication. The method may be in humor, situation comedy, drama, etc.

The mind manipulators often choose the method of the situation comedy to deliver their intended message. The sitcom is loosely based on everyday life and shows the problems that we human beings face and how the characters respond to them and solve them. Some of these shows have been rightly used and have served as role models for the decent trends in television programming.

A myriad of situation comedies and made-for-television movies, along with a glut of day-time soap operas, have been used to preach the doctrine and promote the life-style of the amoral permissiveness espoused by secular humanism. The life-style portrayed on the programs and the characters played have become role models for millions of people. Even one night's viewing will show you that morality is often ridiculed, home and family denigrated — while adultery, homosexuality, dishonesty, incest, child sex, prostitution, pornography, and lust are pictured as normal and desirable.

Or the method may be humor in the form of the "stand-up comic." Take, for example, the remarks by Johnny Carson on NBC's "Tonight Show" when he told a joke about Anita Bryant.

I don't know if there is any direct connection or not, but I saw Rod McKuen, the poet, tell an interviewer on a television program that he was going to contact every comedy writer he knew and ask them to write jokes about Anita Bryant in an effort to ridicule her for her stand against homosexuality.

When you use humor, you don't have to rely on reason or intelligence or fairness to make your point. You bypass the intelligence of the listener and simply appeal to his predilection for prejudice toward all those who disagree with you. It has much the same appeal that the ethnic joke has. You seek to picture the person who disagrees with your views as being so ridiculous as to be unworthy of serious consideration.

Mr. Carson's "joke" made Anita Bryant appear as an object worthy of ridicule. She became laughable. And while the audience responded to his inane remarks with uproarious laughter, the writers of the material must have smiled and congratulated themselves, for they had sent their message over the entire NBC television network — straight into the minds of millions of Americans. The damage was done!

Johnny Carson has prejudiced his viewers against a gallant lady who stood up for decency in the face of a disgusted moral blight in her community. She spoke out against the homosexuals having free access to the minds of her children. And for this she was rewarded with the brand of being "intolerant," "bigoted," "narrow-minded," and wanting to "force her moral values on everyone else."

The tragedy was — many believed him.

The joke carried a much weightier message — a warning — and it sank into the subconscious minds of millions. The message to the rest of us was to beware about what we say or do, or we too will fall victim to the art of propaganda by comedy.

Consider the impact also of the *dramatic* program in presenting ideas to the minds of the audience. We all know the experience of sitting in front of our television sets, totally engrossed in the dramatic unfolding of a story. We become enmeshed in it, unaware even of our surroundings, loving and hating the characters, making irrational judgements as to right or wrong, mesmerized by the genius of manipulation. We become emotionally involved, excited, and entertained.

You are now at your highest point of vulnerability, and the authors and directors can now send you the "message" they want you to receive. You will receive it, and it will influence your thinking. While you sit there in a passive, uncritical attitude, watching and listening, you have opened the door to almost total access to your subconscious mind. The media people know it — and they exploit it.

Before you toss this information aside and say there is no proof that we are being consciously and deliberately manipulated by the people who control what the American people see on television, consider the facts revealed in a recent report published in *Public Opinion*, a magazine of The American Institute for Public Policy Research in Washington, D.C.

The report was written by the research team of Robert Lichter, political scientist at George Washington University; Stanley Rothman, professor at Smith College; and Linda Lichter, research associate at George Washington University. The findings are the result of detailed interviews with 104 of the television elite. In fact, they bothered to interview only people who were associated with two or more successful prime time series, including ". . . some of the most experienced and respected members of the craft. Many have been honored with Emmy Awards, and a few are household names."

As I read through the report, a very clear profile of these people began to emerge, and I didn't like what I was seeing. The information showed that the people who create and control the entertainment seen nightly on television are "overwhelmingly secular in outlook, politicaly liberal, and avoid religion," and that their position on religion and moral values is out of step with the beliefs and attitudes of the vast majority of Americans. Unfortunately, the study also reveals that "this group has had a major role in shaping the shows whose themes and stars have become staples in our popular culture."

Just what do these people believe and what is their values system? Well, the survey gives us definite answers, leaving no room for speculation.

Here are some of the things uncovered: (1) While nearly all of them came out of religious backgrounds, 45 percent now say they have no religion; (2) only 7 percent of them attend a religious service as much as once a month; (3) 80 percent of them do not regard homosexual relations as wrong; (4) 86 percent support the rights of homosexuals to teach in public schools; (5) 51 percent refuse to condemn adultery as wrong; (6) almost all of them — 97 percent — are pro-abortion; (7) 67 percent think that the government should redistribute the income in America, even though 25 percent of them earn more than $500,000 per year, while only 4 percent earn less than $75,000 per year.

It's plain and simple; these people who control

enormous powers over the thought processes of millions of Americans are enemies to the Christian faith.
If you doubt that they are enemies to Jesus Christ,
consider the statement in the survey which says, "It
would be difficult to overestimate the clash of values
when television's creative community confronts fundamentalist Christian critics. Their value orientation
is fundamentally different from that of the general
public . . . they reflect the criticism that television is
too critical of traditional values by an eight-to-one
margin."

The results of this study do not surprise me, but
there was one conclusion that disturbed me a great
deal and should sound an alarm for all Americans.
The fact that these "entertainment" elitists' positions
on religion and moral values is at odds with the overwhelming majority of Americans does not stop them
from imposing their moral value system upon us all.

To the contrary! The survey revealed that ". . .
according to television's creators, they are not in
it just for the money — **they seek to move their
audience toward their vision of the good
society."**

Their version of the "good society" can be summed
up in two words — secular humanism. And it is being
preached daily to millions through drama, situation
comedies, science programs, documentaries, talk
shows, and all other forms of "entertainment."

THE KINGS OF TV

The questions that kept coming back to me again
and again were "**Who decides what will be sent over**

television into the homes? Who determines what the American viewing public will see?"

One day I read an article that settled the question. Ben Stein, lawyer, novelist and TV columnist, said in "The View From Sunset Boulevard," "In television, the producers and writers are creative kings. What they say is law, and that law is transmitted on the airwaves into millions of homes. Television is not necessarily a mirror of anything besides what those few people think."

He then stated that fewer than four hundred people determine what is seen in the sitcoms and adventure shows, which constitute the major part and most influential aspect of TV programming. He further asserted that these same powerful writers are people who are deliberately using our most powerful communications medium to **promote their own social and political views.**

Tragically, every night of the week millions of entertained or amused viewers surrender their thought processes to this medium. Unknowingly, they are receiving the unfiltered messages of the show's braintrust. The programs are telling you what is right and wrong, knowing that you will eventually accept it and integrate it into your own value system. You are being "controlled" under the guise of being entertained.

Please understand that not all shows are designed to indoctrinate, and not all people in show business are trying to seduce you — but many are!

You should be asking, "What will be the long-term effect on our society of this pervasive, humanistic, national electronic brainwash?"

I am fascinated by the modern developments in communications. I believe that all these technological advances should be used to spread the gospel of Christ and do good for mankind. But considering the astounding developments in the fields of communication and information, and considering the impact of these changes on every part of our human existence, it should be clear to everyone that the potential for good or evil is almost unlimited. The communications revolution has given the purveyors of ideas the means to "force-feed" a nation a daily ration of information that almost saturates their thoughts and senses.

Further evidence of the power of the media to affect the minds of people was given in the book *Subliminal Seduction*, when the author said, "The TV machine regulates time, channelizes or unifies perceptual experience and establishes (all subliminally) an entire range of human expectations, value systems, identities, relationships, and perspectives toward the entire world. There exists no single or multiple mechanism available to modern man which holds such a devastating potential for brainwashing, mass programming, and the destruction of individualism — with, of course, reinforcement from the other mass media. This threat is every bit as disastrous for the future of mankind as is pollution, overpopulations, or atomic and biological warfare . . . experiments have established most emphatically that as a . . . brainwashing or conditioning device, television has an enormous potential."

Can you imagine the number of "imprints" made upon your brain in an average day from newspaper ads, billboards, radio and television commercials, and a profusion of other messages that vie for your attention? With such a rash of information, is it any wonder that many people find it difficult to cope in our modern society? This "overload" of information plays a major role in the breakdown of the resistance of the mind, causing it to become passive — no longer able to resist. The person is then "told" what he is to do. He is no longer able, nor does he wish, to resist the pressure to conform.

It is sobering to realize that the media have become so pervasive that to a great extent they determine what we talk about, how we pattern our lives, how we dress, what we buy, how we think. And they shape our political, religious and moral views of life. The simple fact is that if we hope to maintain even a modicum of mental health, spiritual balance, and moral purity, we must become more critical of the media.

THERE'S MORE THAN MEETS THE EAR

It was a cool, brisk day as I drove east on Northwest Highway in Dallas toward the KVTT studios for my broadcast. The twenty minute drive always gives me an opportunity to focus my attention on the upcoming interview. As usual, I didn't know quite what to expect. My guest was going to discuss rock music, so I thought I would do a little "research" while driving. I dialed in one of Dallas' rock stations, and after having my senses assaulted for about six minutes I turned it off and muttered, "That stuff will loosen the fillings in your teeth." So much for the research.

But — I would learn that day that rock music was another powerful psychological weapon in Satan's war for the mind. It was part of the vast program of media manipulation.

Until recently, the messages being preached through the words and music of the rock groups had gone unnoticed by everyone but a few. Even now the average American parent has little or no knowledge of what these groups are saying, or of their devastating effect upon impressionable young minds. Most parents have never bothered to check out the record albums their children are bringing home. Their standard reaction is to shout over the loud, thunderous beat blasting through the walls of the house, **"Turn that noise down!"**

Like most parents, I had heard some of this music and found it to be too loud, irritating and offensive, but I had simply reasoned that this was part of the generation gap. After all, I had been young once, and I enjoyed turning up the music to close out the world and create my own little environment right in my own room. So — I didn't particularly approve of it. Big deal! But why should I mind? And though I didn't completely approve of it, I didn't see why I should get uptight over it.

After all — it was harmless. Or was it?

As had happened so often before, I was to receive an "education" on my own broadcast — on the air — along with thousands of others. I was to be shocked into facing the facts.

I had heard of a young man, Mike Johnson, who himself had been into rock music, but was now speaking out against it in churches and schools. He sounded like a young man who knew what he was talking about, so I invited him to appear on "Point of View."

What I was to see and hear was going to open my eyes to yet another method that was being used to pervert the thinking of the American young people. The information he brought was so astonishing that it was almost unbelievable. But he had his facts together. The proof was in front of me. It was printed on the albums themselves for me to read.

When we were on the air, I introduced Mike and asked him why he objected to much of the contemporary rock music. He told us that many of the rock groups' personal life-styles and philosophies included such things as satanism, sado-masochism, the drug culture, hedonism, homosexuality, bestiality, rebellion, anarchy — and a few lesser evils!

He had my attention!

Mike told us that before he saw the dangers in rock music, he was "hooked" on the Beatles and was quite surprised to learn they had admitted they frequently used drugs and that their songs were replete with references to drug use.

He said that his research had uncovered some other revealing things:

> Derek Taylor (the Beatles' press officer) said, "They're completely anti-Christ. I mean, I am anti-Christ as well, but they're so anti-Christ, they shock me, which isn't an easy thing" (*Saturday Evening Post*, August 1964).

> Paul McCartney said, "We probably seem to be anti-religious because of the fact that none of us believe in God" (*Playboy*, February 1965). The late John Lennon said, "Christianity will go. We're more popular than Jesus now" (*Newsweek*, 1966).

> George Harrison was a follower of the Maharishi Mahesh Yogi and a practicing Hindu as early as 1967. His popular song "My Sweet Lord" was dedicated to Lord Krishna (*Rock*, Bob Larson).

Mike continued to give us documented proof of the perverse nature of these groups:

The group *The Village People* was formed by
Jacques Morali, who said, "I formed this group
as a personal protest against Anita Bryant and to
make gays (homosexuals) more acceptable in
our society" (*Newsweek*, April 2, 1979).

Queen is another group with sexual overtones.
The name Queen is the "drag" overtone of the
word "homosexual." Lead singer Freddy Mercury said, "We want to shock and outrage" (*Circus*, 1975). He appears on stage with his own
brand of purple fingernail polish, mascara and
tight leotards to flaunt his bisexuality and sings,
"We are the Champions" which has been widely
interpreted as the national anthem for the Gay
Liberation Movement. Mercury said, "On stage,
I'm a devil. I think I may go mad in several years'
time" (*Circus,* 1977).

I must admit that what had seemed relatively harmless to me in the past was now beginning to take on an
ominous new meaning. Here were very popular groups
promoting, among other things, sexual perversions. I
thought, "Could there be any doubt in anyone's mind
that thousands of young people are being **recruited** to
enter this life-style by these groups and their songs?"

OCCULTIC ROCK

I was interested in a statement Mike had made
earlier in the show about the influence of the occult on
these groups, and asked him to comment. He shuffled
through the rock albums lying on the table and showed
me one by the group Blue Oyster Cult. On their

"Agents of Fortune" album was a man holding tarot cards (fortune telling), which when decoded read "The one who comes against the power faces death." Mike pointed out to me that the man's other hand points at the satanic cross to show what that power is.

He continued, "Their album 'Fire of the Unknown Origin' flaunts people with different occultic symbols on their foreheads and garments. The album is advertised in rock journals by saying 'Following the Occult.' "

He continued: "Another group, The Eagles, got their name from the major spirit in the Indian cosmos and is based on the teaching of the occultic writer Carlos Casteneda. Their song 'One of These Nights' says, 'You've got your demons, you've got desires, and I've got a few of my own.' Other occultic songs include 'Take the Devil,' 'Journey of the Sorcerer,' 'Witchy Woman,' 'Good Day in Hell,' and 'Hotel California.' "

As I sat there dumbfounded, Mike continued to call the names of the various rock groups and give brief descriptions of their philosophies and how those beliefs are integrated into their songs and music, making them an enormously effective brainwash mechanism. I remember when some eighty thousand people were jammed into the Cotton Bowl in Dallas, Texas to hear the Rolling Stones. It was dramatic testimony to the power these groups exert over the minds of millions in this nation.

Mike continued his expose by saying, "Black Sabbath has a member, Bill Ward, who said, 'Satan could be God' (*Circus,* December 1971). Their bass player, Geezer, said, 'I can see the devil and I'm Lucifer; it's a Satanic world'(*Rolling Stone,* October

1971).

"Former drummer Peter Criss, of Kiss, said, 'I find myself evil. I believe in the devil as much as God. You can use either one to get things done' (*Rolling Stone,* April 1977).

"Parts of the Rolling Stone's album *Goats Head Soup* were recorded live at a Haitian voodoo ritual. One album has the group posed as warlocks on the album cover and is entitled 'Your Satanic Majesty's Request.' The song 'Sympathy For The Devil' is the unofficial national anthem for the satanic groups in America. And in a live concert, Mick is seen wearing a shirt that has Christ hanging upside down on the cross, overshadowed by a Nazi swastika. Earth, Wind and Fire usually join hands before each concert to enter into the proper transcendent state (*Circus,* January 1977). The leader, Maurice White, is a practicing Buddhist (*Rolling Stone,* January 1978), and their song 'Serpentine Fire' is based on the Spinal Life Energy System found in the Shah Kriza Yogi meditation cult. Their album 'All n' All' portrays a cross on the same level as other occultic, religious, and demonic symbols on the inside cover."

After presenting all this information, Mike said, "So you see, Marlin, the occultic doctrine comes through loud and clear in many of these rock songs. And when kids listen to them they are being brainwashed and indoctrinated with its message. Many have turned to the occult through listening to these groups."

Our minds had already been "blown," but the information that was to come was even more frightening. My guest introduced us to a recording technique known as **backward masking.** He explained that this is a technique used by some of the rock groups to "implant" messages into their songs. It is a technique of so arranging the words in the songs that playing the records backward would reveal imbedded messages.

Mike had devised a way to play the records backward so that the message could be heard. He demonstrated this by playing several brief excerpts from several of the albums — backwards — revealing some very astounding things. Some of the phrases and sentences were quite distinguishable when played in this manner. (Mike warned the listeners that this is very rarely used and for people not to let their imaginations run wild).

One of the songs he demonstrated was by Queen, entitled "Another One Bites The Dust." When it was played backward we could hear the phrase "We decided to smoke marijuana."

Mike said "The group Black Oak Arkansas has disbanded, with every veteran of the group now confessing Jesus as Lord, except for the lead singer, Jim Dandy. Their live album Raunch n' Roll, which was produced several years ago, has one song entitled 'The Day Electricity Came To Arkansas.' Halfway through the song, Dandy has the band quiet down and then proceeds to say a meaningless phrase, which when played backwards announces, 'Satan, Satan. He is God. He is God.' It is followed by a sickly, demonic laugh."

When I asked him about the effectiveness of backwards masking, he said that he knew kids who had actually picked up the backwards messages when they were "high" on drugs, even though they could not hear them when they were sober.

The effectiveness of this method of subliminal suggestion (backwards masking) is not fully understood, but some psychologists believe that even though the conscious mind may not pick up the words that are being heard backwards, there is the distinct possibility that the subconscious mind may be able to receive them and translate them into meaning.

MORE THAN MEETS THE EYE

When we opened the telephone lines for people to call in and ask questions, a young man asked about the influence of the movies and asked if my guest saw any danger in them. Mike replied, "In my study of the trend of the movies, I believe they are being used to indoctrinate the kids toward an anti-Christ attitude, especially the science fiction movies. The most popular movies among young people are movies such as *Star Wars, The Empire Strikes Back, Star Trek, The Black Hole,* etc. These are all science fiction, futuristic-type shows."

Mike pointed out that George Lucas, producer of *Star Wars,* said, "The Force is not a malevolent or benevolent thing. It has a good side to it which includes love, charity, fairness and hope. If you use it well you can see the future and the past. You can sort of read minds and you can levitate and use that whole netherworld of psychic energy" *(Time,* 1980).

My guest continued, "The newer movie, *Raiders of the Lost Ark,* was produced by Lucas and Spielberg. When asked if a 'Force' would underlie the Indiana Jones (*Raiders*) movies, Lucas responded in *Rolling* Stone: '*Raiders* will be the most action-oriented of the Indiana Jones movies — the others **should deal more with the occult.**' "

I think thousands of people were beginning to understand that when they went to the movies they were getting more than "entertainment." They were getting indoctrinated with heavy doses of Eastern mysticism and the occult — and making multi-millionaires of the producers in the process. Long gone were the days when you could distinguish the "good" guys from the "bad;" now the theaters are **halls of indoctrination!**

By this time the telephone lines at the radio station were jammed with people who wanted more information. Young people were upset, disturbed, "victimized." They had been subjected to indoctrination through rock music and movies, and they didn't like it! As the result of that interview, hundreds of young people burned and destroyed thousands of dollars worth of rock albums. People began writing for copies of the interview on cassette tapes to share with others or to mail across the country. Our office has mailed thousands of cassette tapes of the interview to parents, teenagers, youth groups, pastors, schools, and churches all across the nation. The effect of this expose of the sinister and satanic influence on rock music and movies has had a dramatic impact on the lives of thousands.

4

SEXUAL EXPLOITATION

It should be apparent to everyone that America is in the throes of a sexual revolution. The "gospel" of the new "sexual freedom" is preached daily through the mass media. The "message" is that men and women have been "liberated" from the restraints of the antiquated Christian moral codes. And, ever-increasing pressure taunts us all to adopt a new national attitude toward sex. Movie stars, rock stars, television personalities, and others flaunt and promote their deviant secular life-styles for the young to adopt and mimic. Sexually explicit television programs and movies paint a picture of sex as being a recreational sport with no responsibilities and no enduring consequences.

Because the American people have failed to train their children in even the rudimentary moral guidelines to their sexuality, and have failed to teach them that sexual abstinence before marriage is right and best for their own benefit, health, and well-being, we're now suffering the consequences with an epidemic of unwanted pregnancies, venereal disease, and tragically ruined lives.

It is into this moral vacuum that the government has entered to train our children to approach sex with the humanistic value system.

Most parents assume that when the school determines to include sex education in its curriculum, the teachers will simply acquaint the students with facts about reproduction and the physical differences between boys and girls. However, humanistic behavioral psychologists, who advocate *total sexual freedom,* have written most of the textbooks, and these textbooks reflect their own humanistic moral values.

When I was interviewing Jo Ann McAuley, she shoved a book in front of me and told me that it was a teacher's guide for a sex education class. She told me to read a few of the lines. What I read so shocked me that I determined — then and there — that I would pursue an investigation of the sex education movement, the organizations pushing it, and the publishing companies publishing the sex education material being used in the classrooms of America.

When the radio listening audience learned that I was investigating sex education, they mailed me enormous amounts of literature, textbooks, slides, teacher training material, etc. As I waded through this material I received a genuine "education." What I discovered appalled me.

The material that came into my hands, plus the interviews I had with educators and concerned parents, uncovered an ideological web of people, politicians, foundations, businesses, the media, and government agencies that were part of an intense movement to erase the Christian principles of sexual morality from this nation and install in their place the "free, liberated sex" immorality of secular humanism.

One of the saddest parts of my investigation, however, was that many Christian ministers, educators, and parents simply *refused to face the facts.* They cannot bring themselves to believe that the public schools' innocuous sex education program could possibly be designed to undermine the Christian morality of their children. On the other hand, I have talked to many parents who finally "woke up" after their children had already adopted the humanistic sexual lifestyle.

The humanists know that the American public must be "re-educated" before they can erase Christian morality regarding sex. In order to do this, they must be employed in such a manner as to mean something different from what the American public has always believed. Nowhere do the humanist propagandists do a more masterful job at interjecting reverse meaning into words than when they discuss sexual morality.

For example, the humanists accuse the Christian of being "sexually immature" and "unsophisticated" in matters relating to sex because he accepts the biblical moral guidelines. However, nothing could be further from the truth. The Christian attitude toward sex is one of a *mature, disciplined* nature. The enlightened Christian knows that God gave mankind the gift of sex not only for procreation but that two people may, in truth, become one. The Scriptures teach that a man and a woman, in holy matrimony, "become one flesh." Two people become one in heart, in mind, in spirit. Any mature, happily married person will verify that true sexual intimacy and sexual pleasure come when this oneness is achieved.

Contrary to humanist propaganda, the Bible does not teach — nor does the Christian believe — that sex is *wrong, dirty or sinful.* The Bible plainly teaches that sexual intercourse between a husband and wife is a gift from God and is right and beautiful. The problem comes when sex is misused, perverted, or misunderstood.

Tragically, Christian parents and the church have abdicated their place of authority and responsibility in factually instructing young people in the biblical use and morality of sex.

And it is in this moral void that the humanists find fertile soil for their indoctrination.

ATTACK ON YOUNG MINDS

In order for the humanists to instill their morality, they must first erase any remaining respect for Christian moral absolutes. They do this by denigrating the Christian in a clear choice of derogatory words designed to convey to their subject's mind that the Christian is not "aware" and is "sexually immature" when he objects to the humanist's interpretation of sexual morality.

There is little hope of changing the sense of right and wrong concerning sex in the minds of the older generation of Americans. So if the humanists are to be successful they must look elsewhere — to the boys and girls!

The battleground will be the public schools.

The strategy — sex education!

With this in mind, you can readily see why the humanist movement is pressing so hard to get sex education into the public schools. You can be assured that sex education will be taught from the amoral standpoint of the *Humanist Manifestos* — **not from the Bible.**

Wardel B. Pomeroy has authored several books now being used in many school districts in their sex education classes. In his book *Girls And Sex*, he expressed the opinion that there is no such thing as "normal sex." He states, "All mammals, of which human beings are a species, engage in practically every kind of sex, including petting, masturbation and homosexuality, so there is essentially nothing humans do sexually that is abnormal." He further suggests that "our society makes altogether too much out of the problem of premaritial intercourse."

In Mr. Pomeroy's book *Your Child And Sex: A Guide For Parents,* he declares, "Modesty is a learned behavior, drummed into the skulls of children, dictated in the Western world by the Judeo-Christian culture and its code of behavior . . . "

I was not altogether surprised to read that Mr. Pomeroy condemned Christian morality and then praised the "enlightened parents" whose son "thoughtfully" explained that on a weekend boat trip with his parents he wanted to bring a friend who was homosexual. He then explained that he was a homosexual too, and they expected to sleep together on the trip. So the "enlightened" parents consented to let him come as long as he was "congenial" on the trip.

This approach to sex is nothing short of mental and moral "rape" of the child's mind. It conveys a distorted, perverted view of sex, confusing his values and presenting information he is not mature enough to handle. And it has the power and prestige of the classroom, school system, and teacher reinforcing it. The child is overwhelmed.

But, of course, if you are a parent and you speak up

against this "enlightened" kind of sex education, you will be immediately branded as a "reactionary" and will suffer hostility from the more "mature" humanists.

Another little "gem" of a textbook approved in a number of states is *Person To Person.* Chapter 12 discusses "Changing Life Styles" and devotes an entire illustrated page to discussion of renewable or contract marriages, which "allow a couple the option of renewing their marriage every five years." To make the idea palatable to young minds, an illustration is given for just how it would work: "The renewable marriage contract is one effort to remove some of the trauma and trouble caused by reaching a decision to divorce . . . Lester and Naomi decided to enter into a contract marriage. They felt that their feelings for each other were solid enough to form a good marriage. On the other hand, they felt they would be cheating themselves if they assumed their feelings would last a lifetime. Therefore, they agreed to marriage renewable every five years. They renewed their private marriage contract twice, but decided not to renew it after they had been married fifteen years."

It sounds to me like a case of "lease-a-wife" instead of a lifetime commitment. Is there any question that "values" are being taught? These are the values not of the Christian but of secular humanism.

Sol Gordon, professor of Child and Family Studies at *Syracuse University,* Syracuse, N.Y., is author of much of the material being used in the sex education classes across America. One of the guests on "Point of View" showed me some of his material, including his "sex comic book." It was offensive to anyone who had even a modicum of morality; yet it is being used to teach children about sex.

In a speech at the New York City Health Education Conferences, Gordon suggested that those who oppose his ideas of sex education in the classroom demonstrate that they believe knowledge is harmful. He stated, "It is not enough to teach biological realities. You must also have values. Our values must be moral ... our values must **not be religious**, but rather those of the **universal aspirations of the society we live in. We must insist on democratic values! And that's what** we must teach our children, so that they carry on the fight against fascism and communism **and religious intolerance!** And whenever we find values opposed to our own, the truly transcendent ones, **we must root them out, so that freedom will reign.**"

Sex education should be called sexual seduction of the minds of the children by the humanists.

Each parent should do his own research into the philosophy of those writers and publishers who are furnishing the textbooks and teachers' guides for the sex education classes to be taught in the public schools. Once you understand the system of teaching known as "values clarification" and what its purpose is, you will be able to spot many incidents of its use in various school curricula, including sex education. My research has revealed that practically all the material — the textbooks, workbooks, movies, slides — used in sex education classes reflect the amoral, humanistic attitude toward sex.

And your child will reflect this attitude in his lifestyle if he is subjected to it.

SIECUS: FOUNTAIN OF PERVERSION

An overwhelming preponderance of the nation's sex education material comes from Sex Information and Education Council of the United States (SIECUS). Incidentally, its president, Dr. Mary Calderone, was named "Humanist of the Year" for 1974. Her statement on "sexual experimentation" reflects her amoral, humanistic attitude: "The adolescent years are, among other things, for learning how to integrate sex usefully and creatively into daily living. Therefore, we must accept that adolescent sexual experimentation is not just inevitable, but actually necessary for normal development."

Her views on premarital sex also reflect this same value system. She states: "I advocate discussion of it, so that young people know they have choices beginning with masturbation, of course, and petting to climax and mutual orgasm before moving on to intercourse."

I had once heard a wise minister say, "We are always just one generation away from the jungle." And secular humanism is laboring hard to lower us to the morality of jungle life. They have zeroed in on the children and young people of our nation, hoping to subvert that one generation that will bring about their goals. They are turning them away from God to the worship of self, reducing them to the common denominator of their "sexual parts," encouraging them to cast aside all moral restraints, and indulge themselves in a life-long search for "pleasure" through drugs, animalistic sex and any other form of pleasure that may promise a physical, spiritual or mental "orgasm."

Some of the material that I uncovered included descriptions and instructions on how to use contraceptives, and even seventh-grade-level curriculum used such terms as vagina, nocturnal emission, ejaculation, and erection, along with graphic pictures of persons in various sexual poses. It should be evident to any intellectually honest adult that this is pretty heavy stuff, and that such open discussion — in a mixed-class setting — desensitizes the students to the private and personal nature of their own sexual organs and feelings. Teenagers have told me that they have felt peer pressure to experiment with sexual intercourse as the result of having been in the sex education class with those of the opposite sex.

Most of the authors of this material are active, militant humanists, and many of them traverse this nation, appearing on talk shows and college campuses, preaching the good news of humanistic "sexual liberation." And even though they loudly proclaim that sex will be taught on a non-moral basis, the truth of the matter is that the curriculum substitutes the humanistic ethic for traditional values.

I was asked to appear, along with several others, at a Dallas television show to discuss the subject of sex education in the public schools. There were several who spoke for each point of view. The program was lively, with each side taking its best shots. I was rather amused at a gentlemen who identified himself as a teacher who was teaching a sex education class in a Dallas public school. He wanted to "set us straight" as to what was being taught in the classroom. He had no doubt that his explanation would clear the air and resolve this silly controversy once and for all.

Methodically, he outlined his subject material and then pronounced that he taught on a "non-moral" basis and encouraged his students to "make up their own minds" about whether or not to engage in sexual intercourse before marriage. He said that he felt this was the "open-minded" approach to the subject.

What the teacher didn't realize — and we were kind

enough to "enlighten" him — was that he was giving the students a good dose of situational ethics and was instilling within them the conclusion that there were no "moral absolutes" to guide them. He was indoctrinating them with humanism — **and he honestly did not know he was doing it!**

It is such brainwashing, in hundreds of cases across America, that entices young people to approach sex from a non-moral standpoint, leading to adolescent experimentation and shattered lives.

HUMANISM'S SEXUAL GOALS

This sexual revolution did not come about accidentally. It is part of the plan to secularize this nation. *Humanist Manifesto II* is very explicit about the goals to change the sexual moral concepts in America. Affirmation Six states:

In the area of sexuality, we believe that intolerant attitudes often culivated by orthodox religions and puritanical cultures unduly repress sexual conduct. The right to birth control, abortion, and divorce should be recognized. While we do not approve of exploitative denigrating forms of sexual expression, neither do we wish to prohibit, by law or social sanction, sexual behavior between consenting adults. The many varieties of sexual exploration should not in themselves be considered evil. Short of harming others or compelling them to do likewise, individuals should be permitted to express their sexual proclivities and pursue their lifestyles as they desire. Moral education for children and adults is an important way of developing awareness and sexual maturity.

The humanist creates his own system of moral values, and then accuses those who disagree with him of having "intolerant attitudes" or of being "puritanical," while describing his own attitudes as being "open-minded" and "tolerant." Further, this document reveals their intention of propagandizing our nation with this moral doctrine, for they plainly state, "Moral education for children and adults is an important way of developing awareness and sexual maturity." When humanists speak of "moral education," they are speaking of the immorality of humanism not of the morals of the Bible. In their view, any person who subscribes to the morality of the Bible is "sexually immature" and in need of "having his awareness and sexual maturity developed"; and they fully intend to furnish you with that "education."

The belief that sex should be confined to marriage is ludicrous to the humanist mind. Consequently, we have marriages of convenience, with a large part of our populace unable to have real relationships. Instead, they are lost and lonely. Christianity, on the other hand, is based on lasting and enduring relationships — first to God; then to family; and then to those around us. While the human heart longs for a close relationship with another human being, casual and free sex destroys any possibility of this developing.

We are all sexual beings. God made us that way. Sex within the confines of marriage is honorable. When we try to understand a person's craving for sexual experience, we must not separate it from the essential need for intimacy. When intimacy is not achieved in a normal, healthy way people often turn to pornography, homosexuality, bestiality, and other forms of sexual perversion.

NEW SEX LAWS

This nation has seen within the last few years a plethora of proposed legislation promoted by humanist front organizations, intended to bring the laws of the land into line with their doctrines. Laws that do not agree with their position are termed "intolerant attitudes often cultivated by orthodox religions" and "puritanical cultures." Furthermore, they say that these antiquated laws "unduly repress sexual conduct." The humanist movement is constantly pushing for legislation that would make their concept of right and wrong, including laws that concern sexual behavior, become the laws of the land.

Their Manifesto reveals the depravity of their minds, and they wish to impose their moral sickness on us all through the force of the law. If they are successful in their efforts, social and moral restraints would be lifted, and practically anything that a degenerate mind could conceive would be considered socially acceptable. All the laws of the land that are based on the Judeo-Christian moral code would be struck down, and we would experience a sexual degeneration that would cause Sodom and Gomorrah to look like a weekend at Disneyland.

Dr. Corliss Lamont, a humanist and devout atheist, summed up the humanist concept of sex and morality when he said, "Morally speaking, **the sex life of an individual is no more important than his political or economic life.**"

Can the American public continue to be so naive as to believe that there is no concerted, humanist effort to bring about a sexual revolution in this nation? Can we continue to close our eyes to the encroachment of homosexuality on our school textbooks? These people are adept at disguising their true intentions behind a facade of secularistic do-goodism, but they will rob your child of his sexual identity and tell him they are helping him to "clarify" his own values.

Your child is not immune to this insidious brainwash. And the cutting edge of this sexual propaganda blitz is the sex education of our public schools.

Thousands of children are being subjected to homosexual propaganda under the guise of sex education. For example, many schools are showing a film that deals with lesbianism. The film is entitled *Lavender.* It is intended to "de-sensitize" children to the subject of lesbianism.

The "Suggested Uses and Discussion Topics" section of its promotional pamphlet explains that *Lavender* is a very useful film in "gently, yet openly, introducing high school students to this delicate area of sexuality." It can also "be very helpful in relieving the many misunderstandings and fears that accompany new-found adolescent emotions." Here are questions which can be raised: (1) How can the student better understand and deal with the natural and yet frightening feelings they have for their peers? (2) What sort of attitude did they have toward homosexuality and lesbianism before? (3) Has the film opened up any new areas of thought?

In case there were any lingering doubts about the full intentions of the film, the pamphlet includes a little insight into the motives of the film's producer by saying, " She strongly believes that the film can be used to re-educate and responsibly influence social patterns . . . " (emphasis added).

At this point, I don't think there can be any doubt that the purpose of the film is to recruit young people into the homosexual life-style. And it's being done at your schools — with your tax dollars.

ATTACK ON THE FAMILY

When Dee Jepsen, wife of Senator Roger Jepsen (R-Iowa), appeared as my guest on "Point of View," she expressed both her and her husband's concern over the frontal attack on the family. She placed in my hand a news release from her husband's office in Washington, D.C., which explained that Senators Jepsen and Paul Laxalt (R-Nev.) and Rep. Albert Lee Smith (R-Ala.) had introduced the Family Protection Act of 1981 to tackle the problems that surround government intervention in the lives of individuals and their families.

At a news conference, Senator Jepsen said, "The family unit is so basic, so fundamental and so necessary to society that it is hard to believe that it is under attack — but it is. The family has become a favorite target for some organizations and people bent on transforming the existing social order. With the accelerated erosion of the basic family values due to government intrusion and growing secular humanism, the time for 'family protection' legislation has arrived."

It seems ludicrous to thinking individuals that a government designed to protect the most sacred of institutions — the family — would have to enact special legislation to restrain that same government from seeking to destroy it. But, the fact of the matter is — **the family is indeed threatened!**

The humanists, seeking to bring about a secular society, have been extremely effective in infiltrating — and gaining control of — many organizations and influencing them to fall into step with their plans to bring about their dreamed-of "sexless society."

A case in point is the 1970 White House Conference on Children and Youth, which spawned the Forum 14 Report that "redefined" the family as a **"group of individuals in interaction."** The American Home Economics Associations, in an attempt to mollify public sentiment against such changes, couched their new definition of the family in the words "(the family is) **a unit of two or more persons who share values and have a commitment to one another over time."**

These definitions, if enacted into law in the United States, could bring about unthinkable changes in American society. The "family" would include group marriages, homosexual and lesbian marriages, or any other conglomerate of individuals who choose to "interact" over a period of time with some modicum of commitment.

What is wrong with the classical definition of the family that has been traditionally defined thus: "The family is two or more persons related by blood, heterosexual marriage (one man, one woman), or adoption?" It has worked for centuries. Why try to redefine it now? Unless, of course, you want to erase all sexual distinctions in society!

DEATH BY ANY OTHER NAME

When the Supreme Court of the United States ruled on Roe v. Wade, on January 22, 1973, legalizing abortion-on-demand, it put America into the "abortion business." The ruling held that whether or not the unborn child is a human being, **he is not a person** within the meaning of the Fourteenth Amendment. Since the right to life is guaranteed only to "persons," the ruling means that the unborn child, as a non-person, has no constitutional right to life.

Overnight, the most dangerous place for a child became his mother's womb.

One organization representing this new burgeoning abortion business is the Abortion Federation of America, a national association that represents 190 abortion clinics scattered throughout the United States.

Through many years of investigative reporting, I have learned that if you want to get the facts straight, you must go to the person or organization and get them to tell you what they do and what they believe. Get them to talk. Get it first-hand. Then present the facts to the people. I work on the assumption that the people who listen to my broadcast or read what I write are intelligent enough to draw their own conclusions.

So when the Abortion Federation of America came to Dallas for a conference, I tucked my notebook and portable tape recorder under my arm, went to the conference, and told them I wanted to talk to the person who was in charge of the organization.

They introduced me to Dr. Uta Landy, an attractive lady in her 30s, who is executive director of the organization. When she learned that I was with a radio station, she was delighted to have the opportunity to talk to me and express her views.

In the interview Dr. Landy told me that since the Supreme Court decision in 1973, there is an average of one and one-half million abortions performed each year in this nation. About one million of these are performed by clinics that are members of their organization.

As she was talking, I realized that these are the

people who are the very heart and soul of the abortion business!

The interview lasted about forty-five minutes, during which time I was trying to uncover the moral concepts of those who were in the business of terminating human lives. I wanted to hear an explanation of their controlling principles — their value system. I wanted to cut away the facade of respectability and reveal to the public the underlying reasons for their business.

And the answer came through loud and clear — **money!** The abortion business is extremely profitable, grossing **over three billion dollars each year!**

When I got back to my office, I went into our recording studio to review the program. I was stunned at what I was hearing. The full impact of Dr. Landy's interview had not completely penetrated my thinking until I listened to the playback of our conversation. The interview was an incredible expose of the "mindset" of the people in the abortion business. Her usage of certain words and phrases revealed that she had been well schooled in how to use them.

Within the past decade I have noticed the infusion of a completely new language into our society. I call this new language, used by the secular humanists in their attempt to hoodwink the American people, the *new secularistic language!* It is a whole new language that is devised to distort facts, confuse issues and persuade people to believe lies. It is a language **designed to deceive.**

As I listened to Dr. Landy's careful choice of words, I had to admit that she was an expert at employing the new secularistic language. She had received proper education in the words to use, as well as the words to avoid. I jotted down a few of her secularistic double-talk phrases.

The words "unborn child" were never said; the unborn child was always referred to as a "fetus." The word for "life" became "moment of viability." Fornication and adultery became "sexually active." Pregnancy was referred to as a "biological accident." "Abortion" was called a "medical procedure"; "abortion-on-demand" was simply "pro-choice." And, "pro-choice" was rationalized by the question "Why should any woman have to 'suffer' because of a 'biological accident' when a simple 'medical procedure' can eliminate the 'problem'?"

THE NAZI MENTALITY

I kept the interview with Dr. Landy filed away in my office for several months, waiting for the proper time to release it on the air. I chose to broadcast the taped interview on January 22, 1982, on the ninth anniversary of the Supreme Court's decision legalizing abortion-on-demand. The decision to broadcast it on that particular day was prompted by the announcement that some of the abortion clinics in Dallas were giving free abortions in celebration of the anniversary.

Following the playing of the pre-recorded interview with Dr. Landy, I interviewed Dr. William Brennan, who was in the studio with me. Dr. Brennan wrote a book entitled *Medical Holocausts: Exterminative Medicine in Nazi Germany and Contemporary America*. The parallels he drew between Nazi Germany (and the Nazi-mentality that brought the "holocaust" with its inhuman, systematic extermination of millions of Jews and other people) and the present abortion-mentality here in the U.S. were startling.

Dr. Brennan said, "What is happening today in this country has historical precedence. If you want to destroy large numbers of individuals, first, you must have the technology capable of destroying individuals on a mass level. Nazi Germany pioneered mass assembly-line destruction by killing millions of Jews, Gypsies, Poles, asocials and others. Today, we have the same kind of assembly-line technology being directed at the unwanted unborn. Since the Supreme Court decision, upwards of 13 million human lives, before birth, have been destroyed by physicians on an assembly-line basis. This is what makes today a holocaust. You see, if you have the 'technology' which is capable of doing it, and it is perpetrated by credentialed, licensed, 'executioners,' then you can get away with it."

He then paused, leaned a little closer to the microphone, and spoke slowly and deliberately: "You see, Mr. Maddoux, if you are going to destroy millions of individuals, you have to first of all **demean them and reduce them to a level less than human and use derogatory terminology against them — just like the Nazis did!**"

He continued, "Marlin, when I was doing the research I found that the most striking parallel was the 'language' used."

He then handed me an article and said, "This article shows that the California Medical Association in 1970 focused on getting abortion acceptable to the public. They indicated that what they would have to do was to change the Judeo-Christian ethic to a **relative-value-on-human-life ethic.** Their strategy was to call abortion something other that 'killing' and call the unborn child something other than 'human.' Then with the involvement of the medical professional, it would be conducted under socially impeccable auspices and abortion woud have respectability."

I responded by saying, "Then when abortion moved from the back alleys — and the coat hanger — into the sterile operating rooms, surrounded by trained nurses and trusted doctors in white, it became respectable to take human life."

He agreed.

THE NEW MEDICAL ETHIC

After the interview I drove back to my office, where I sat at my desk wondering if the American people had the slightest understanding of the issues before us. The mere possibility of our nation adopting such a moral position was almost beyond consideration. My mind could not grasp such madness.

While sitting there, I picked up the article that Dr. Brennan had given me. Halfway through the article it began to dawn on me that such a system of morality was not as repugnant to others as it was to me. (After I read the article, I had trouble sleeping for several nights, for what I had read came from a prestigious, trusted and respected profession. And if the medical doctors adopted this morality, then millions in our society would say that it must be the right way).

Here are some excerpts from the article that appeared in *California Medicine* in September 1970, entitled " A New Ethic For Medicine And Society." It says: "The traditional Western ethic has always placed great emphasis on the intrinsic worth and equal value of every human life regardless of its stage or condition. This ethic has had the blessings of the Judeo-Christian heritage and has been the basis for

most of our laws and much of our social policy . . .
This traditional ethic is still clearly dominant, but
there is much to suggest that it is being eroded at its
core and may eventually be abandoned. It will become necessary and acceptable to place relative
rather than absolute values on such things as human
lives. In defiance of the long-held Western ethic of
intrinsic and equal value for every human life regardless of its stage, condition or status, abortion is becoming accepted by society as moral, right and even
necessary . . . Since the old ethic has not yet been fully
displaced, **it has been necessary to separate the idea
of abortion from the idea of killing,** which con-
tinues to be socially abhorrent. The result has been a
curious avoidance of the **scientific fact, which everyone really knows,** that human life begins at conception and is continuous, whether intra- or extra-uterine,
until death. The very considerable **semantic gym-
nastics** which are required to rationalize abortion as
anything but taking a human life would be ludicrous
if they were not often put forth under **socially acceptable auspices.** It is suggested that **this schizophrenic
sort of subterfuge** is necessary because **while a new
ethic is being accepted, the old one has not yet been
rejected** . . . One may anticipate further developments of these roles as the problems of **birth control**
and **birth selection** are extended to **death selection**
and **death control** . . ." (emphasis added).

I laid the article down on my desk and spoke out
loud. "This is unbelievable! Humanism has tried to
make man into a 'god'; now he is trying to play the part
of God — deciding who will live and who will be put to
death."

While considering the somber implications of this
new information and wondering how the human race

could have sunk so low, I opened the Bible in front of me; and almost as if God wanted to explain to me why, I read through tear-filled eyes the words of Romans Chapter Three:

Their feet are swift to shed blood!
Ruin and misery mark their ways,
and the way of peace they do not know.
There is no fear of God before their eyes.

I closed the Bible and whispered, "God, please have mercy on the human race."

PLANNED PARENTHOOD

Ann Landers writes a popular advice column that appears in many newspapers across the nation. One letter she printed said, ". . . at age 16 I found Mr. Right. I was sure we would spend the rest of our lives together. After a few months of heavy petting, we drifted into having sex. Birth control was the last thing on my mind. Withdrawal had worked fine for my girlfriends, and if it worked for them, it would work for me. Well, it worked fine until I missed two periods. There was a free abortion clinic in our town. No one knew except my older sister. It would have killed my parents. As for 'Mr. Right,' he dropped me fast — didn't want to get mixed up in anything like that. He thought he was too young for so much responsibility — not too young to have sex every night, just too young to get 'involved.'

"The message I want to get across to all teenagers is this: Don't wait until something like this happens to you before you start to use birth control. An abortion is much more painful and humiliating than going to your mother and telling her you need some advice on how to keep from getting pregnant. And you guys are idiots if you think it's more embarrassing to buy a condom than to take your girl to a doctor to find out if she is pregnant.

"Having an abortion is horrible. I still feel guilty and wonder what the baby would have looked like. Please, kids, listen to me. It can and will happen to you if you keep messing around without protection."

Ann Landers' answer to the young girl was "Some teenagers can't go to their parents for information because they don't have that kind of relationship" (The *Dallas Morning News,* Dce. 21, 1981). She then recommended that they write to Planned Parenthood Federation.

The young girl's letter reflects the heartache and agony brought on by the so-called "sexual revolution" in our country. Her letter said nothing about moral values in regard to sex outside of marriage, or of the morality of abortion. She was simply doing what all her girl friends were doing, and her advice to other young girls was to "get protection."

The columnist's advice to her reflected the humanistic value system. She didn't even suggest that young people should wait until marriage to have sex. Horrors! That would be "judgemental" and forcing your values on someone else. But she did advise her to contact Planned Parenthood, an organization in the forefront of the humanistic sex education movement in our nation.

Even a cursory investigation of Planned Parenthood will reveal its connection to the overall humanist philosophy. For example, Dr. Alan Guttmacher served as Planned Parenthood's president from 1962 until his death in 1974. Is it coincidental that he was a signer of Humanist Manifesto II?

It is obvious that Planned Parenthood is largely humanist-controlled. The link between them and the American Humanist Association shows that it is a tool in helping to bring about the humanist goal. This is clearly revealed in an article in *The Humanist* entitled "Intergroup Relations of the American Humanist Associations," showing that various organizations are philosophically intertwined. It says, "Our humanist convictions should lead us into active participation in specialized organizations devoted to kindred causes. Without neglecting their primary loyalty, humanists and humanist groups should relate to and strengthen such organizations as, for example, the American Civil Liberties Union . . . the Planned Parenthood Federation . . . and Americans United for Separation of Church and State" (The *Humanist,* Jan.-Feb., 1963).

An intriguing picture begins to unfold as you investigate the organizations that are instruments in fulfilling the goals of Humanist Manifestos I and II. As I crosschecked the people and financial backers of these various humanist organizations, I found an incredible overlapping. The same names, the same universities, the same governmental agencies, the same private companies and tax-exempt foundations are linked together in what can only be described as **a humanist conspiracy** to brainwash the American people.

An expose of the marriage of certain financial institutions and the humanist movement is found in the book *The Siecus Circle* (p. 331), revealing that financial support of Planned Parenthood itself has been largely provided by such tax-exempt institutions as the Ford Foundation, which also supports Siecus; the

Commonwealth Fund, another Siecus supporter; and the Victor-Bostrum Fund, which is heavily involved in the population control movement.

They further state: "Various federal agencies are in league with the above foundations. In 1970, grants made by the U.S. Government to Planned Parenthood soared to $1,023,000.00. In fact, the relationship between Planned Parenthood and our government is so close that, of 139 local agency projects initiated by Planned Parenthood's Center For Family Planning Program Development between 1967-1970, ninety-three were funded by federal grants. Planned Parenthood operates the largest abortion clinics in the nation, as well as carrying on extensive education programs which extend into the public schools, offering free contraceptives, abortions and advice on 'problem pregnancies'. And — a large portion of their funding comes from your tax money!"

While talking to Senator Roger Jepsen's wife, Dee, on "Point of View," I suggested to her that I would like to see a full-scale congressional investigation of Planned Parenthood, with special scrutiny of its close ties to other known humanist organizations and of their blatant humanist approach to teaching sex to the students of our public schools. I was delighted to learn that Senators Jeremiah Denton, Don Nickles, and Orin Hatch are leading in the campaign to expose Planned Parenthood's programs and thus eliminate their funding.

According to an Associated Press release (March 29, 1981), Sen. Denton, in an attempt to enlighten the members of Congress, arranged for a showing of the Planned Parenthood film entitled About Sex to the Senate Labor Committee.

The press release stated, "Senator Jeremiah Denton said he would conduct an R-rated hearing on family planning . . . No one under 18 was to be allowed without parents or guardians. The reason, the Alabama republican said, is 'a particular film that will be shown at the hearing used nudity, profanity and explicit sexual language.' Denton was to chair the full Senate Labor Committee hearing on films and other material used in family planning clinics."

Isn't it incredible that the film *About Sex*, by Dr. Sol Gordon, is being shown in many classrooms in schools across the nation to your children, and yet it was closed to those under 18 at the committee hearing. The report is that the senators were shocked at what they saw. And yet many of our elected officials continue to pour millions of dollars into Planned Parenthood and other humanist organizations that are part of the conspiracy to bring a total secular state here in America.

5

TIME FOR
HARD THINKING

When I first began researching the humanist movement in America, I would not believe that there were people in powerful positions who could possibly be involved in a "moral overthrow" of this nation. But as I began to admit to myself that it indeed was true, I also wondered if I were just becoming a "conspiracy nut" who saw a sinister plot in everything that took place. I had heard radicals who screamed about these things but didn't have any facts. However, I now had those "facts" in front of me.

Over the past few years I have interviewed some of the most knowledgeable and informed people in this nation and have read mountains of material published by people with impeccable credentials; and I have had to admit to myself that we are, indeed, fighting for our very survival.

As the enormity of the influence of humanism on

the American culture began to sink into my thinking, I responded with a variety of emotions. There was *regret* — because I had not recognized the root of the problem before; *intimidation* — for I feared there was no hope of turning this country around; *frustration* — for the task of alerting the nation and turning the tide seemed overwhelming; *denial* — because it just couldn't be as bad as some would have us believe; *resignation* — because there was nothing we could do anyway.

These thoughts and emotions pounded my brain night and day for months. I had buried myself in study and research, and it had taken its toll on me spiritually, mentally, and emotionally.

One day I found myself driving toward Addison Airport in the north part of Dallas — out near where I live — just to simply "get away" for a brief time. I had taken up flying many years ago and use it in my ministry as well as a method of relaxation. My children, Mark, David, Tim, and Marla, had flown with me many times when they were younger. My wife, Mary, also enjoys flying, but today I was alone, lost in my thoughts.

Sometimes when I have been struggling with complex issues and making hard decisions, I will escape momentarily by recalling times when life was slower and simpler. While driving, I was remembering the times when my daughter, Marla, was a little girl, and we would sometimes leave the house on a bright, sunshiny day, telling her mother that we were going to "Mickey Mouse" around. It simply meant that we were going to spend time together. Doing nothing special. Going nowhere in particular. With no set time to be home. Just father and daughter — getting acquainted — having fun — talking things over —

building a relationship that would last a lifetime. And when we pulled the car out of the driveway, we would go where we wanted to go and come back when we pleased.

And often we would go to the airport. To watch the airplanes . . . or talk to the pilots.

Or go flying!

But on that day I needed to do some thinking and hold a deep conversation with God. The issues in which I was getting involved were heavy, and I could feel their weight. I needed God's direction and His strength, and the cockpit of my single-engine Cessna 172 often became my private sanctuary.

Before I knew it I was pulling up to the hangar where the orange and white plane is kept. I got out of the car, gave the plane a "pre-flight" check, climbed into the cockpit, shut and locked the door, called out the window "clear the prop," and fired the engine.

After the engine was running smoothly and all the gauges registered "in the green," I picked up the microphone and spoke into it. "Addison Ground Control, this is Cessna Seven-Three-Four-Lima-Kilo, request permission to taxi to active runway."

A disembodied voice crackled over the speaker "Roger, Seven-Three-Four-Lima-Kilo, taxi to runway one-five."

I acknowledged his instructions and with just a touch of power the plane began to roll. I thought to myself that planes are made to fly, not to roll on the ground. On the ground they seem awkward. Within a couple of minutes I was sitting at the run-up area going through my pre-takeoff check list.

Instruments — check! Flight controls — check! Engine run-up — check! Everything was ready to go, so I switched my radio to the tower frequency and said, "Cessan 734LK, ready to go on one-five, north-east departure."

The tower replied, "Lima-Kilo, taxi into position and hold."

I responded by taxiing onto the runway and aligning the plane with the white centerline, and then I heard the tower say, "Seven-Three-Four-Lima-Kilo, cleared for immediate take-off."

After acknowledging his clearance, I eased the throttle forward, and the little four-place plane started down the runway. Full power. Gaining speed. Glance at the airspeed indicator. Thirty knots . . . forty knots . . . fifty knots. At fifty-five knots I gently pulled back on the control wheel and felt the airplane leave the runway.

The sensation still amazed me after more than fifteen hundred hours of flying time. We were leaving the earth. Reaching for the sky. Hold her on the runway heading, then a gentle turn to the left to a heading of zero-two-zero degrees.

Still climbing . . . no hurry. Listen to the engine . . . and the wind. Watch for other planes. Level off at twenty-eight hundred feet until out of the terminal control area, then climb to fifty-five hundred feet. The houses, cars, highways, lakes — all seem miniature from this altitude. Maybe that is why I love to fly. For a brief time I can rise above the world and its problems.

The air is clean . . . there's time to think, to breathe. Time to brush away the cobwebs from my mind. No phones no appointments.

Just me. And my plane . . . and God!

My solitude was broken as I looked down to see Lake Texoma and realized that I had been flying longer than I thought. In the distance was Lake

Texoma Lodge and its small landing strip. I might as well, I thought. So I banked the plane, lost altitude, entered the traffic pattern, and "greased it on" to the runway, thinking *"Why couldn't someone be with me when I make a 'good' landing?"*

I parked the little plane. It's quiet here.

I didn't bother to go to the lodge. Maybe some other time. I just walked around the golf course and over into the woods. Listening to the birds. Watching a hawk soar near the clouds. Smelling the grass. Feeling the wind in my face.

Questions were hanging in my brain. *Unanswered.* The thoughts that kept coming back to my mind like a broken record were "How could I have lived so long and not have seen what was going on? Why hadn't I made the connection before? And what about me? Could my thinking have been influenced by secular humanism? If so, how can I recognize it and how should I go about undoing the damage?

After months of research, investigations, interviews and discussing the issues on radio, television, in public meetings, and privately, I had become convinced that our nation was being subjected to the most intense form of *indoctrination, persuasion* and *national brainwashing* ever attempted on a "free" society.

I could not escape the conclusion that there is an on-going, concerted attempt to re-direct an entire nation of people away from the noble and lofty purposes of its founding fathers; away from a spirit of *freedom, independence, individuality* and *national pride;* and toward an attitude of distrust of patriotism and of acceptance of a "socialistic" and "collectivistic" mentality; and further, that we are being propagandized to reject the basic Judeo-Christian moral value system — and to accept the "humanistic" value system as our foundation for laws and social morality.

I strolled over to a grove of trees, sat down, leaned back against a tree, picked up a blade of grass and put it between my teeth. It had a sweet, fresh taste. The sun was bright and warm.

"Media!" flashed into my mind.

Radio, television, movies, newspapers, magazines — they all seemed to play a part in this national propaganda "blitz." Even many major colleges and universities, much of the entertainment industry, "liberal" theologians, seminaries, churches and denominations, much of our judicial system, and large segments of the United States government seemed to be our enemies in this life-and-death struggle for moral sanity. The odds against us seemed overwhelming.

I had a lot on my mind, so I decided that I would present Him with the question, then be quiet and let Him answer.

I simply said, "What do You want me to do?"

He told me. And I heard Him — in the deep, quiet recesses of my spirit. It became clear. I received direction. Knowing that now I can no longer sit on the sidelines and cheer for those who are in the conflict. I will have to speak out — on radio, on television, in print. I must try to alert, inform, educate, even agitate, if necessary. But the people must be awakened. They must bind themselves together as one body, in harmony, and speak with one voice against the growing influence of evil in this nation.

As I climbed back into the plane and strapped myself in for the flight back to Addison, I felt the calm assurance that God has everything under control.

And I felt my spirit rising to accept the challenge as

God reminded me that the *conflict is spiritual* and that we are to use the powerful weapons of *truth, intercessory prayer,* and the incredible **power of the Holy Spirit.**

THIS MEANS YOU

The humanist world view has greatly influenced the thinking, moral values, and life-styles of millions of people who have never even heard of the Humanist Manifestos. They are living their daily lives totally unaware of the impact that this atheistic, materialistic doctrine has had on them. Sadly, many professed Christians are among that number.

When Tim and Beverly LaHaye were guests on "Point of View," we discussed the influence of humanism on the school, the church, the media, and especially, the home and family. They pointed out that not all people who are influenced by and pattern their lives, to a greater or lesser degree, after the moral code of humanism, are committed humanists.

In reading Tim's book *Battle for the Family* in preparation for the interview, I was impressed by his explanation that ". . . humanism is a philosophical religious movement that has as many differences or degrees as one finds among Christians."

He then gave an enlightening explanation of the levels of influence of, or commitment to, the doctrine of humanism. First, there is the *committed humanist,* who is an indoctrinaire, hardcore, who aggressively pursues humanistic goals, and probably signed Humanist Manifestos I and II. This person may or may not be a Marxist, but he works for liberal causes and opposes moral absolutes. Second, there is the *liberal humanist,* who is a family-oriented, patriotic person who has been exposed to humanism throughout his schooling. This person likes a moral climate in society but does not realize the social consequences of humanism. Third, there is the *humanist victim*, who believes and often lives like a committed humanist, is probably not a Marxist, but does not realize they think alike. He opposes traditional morals as too *restrictive.* Fourth, there is the *Christianized humanist,* who may not be religious although he admires moral values but does not realize these values came from Christianity or Judaism. Fifth, there is the *humanized Christian,* who is a person who is family-oriented, patriotic, and was exposed to humanism throughout his schooling. He has thought very little about religion or moral values, but he likes for his family to be in a moral environment, not knowing that humanist policies will destroy his family.

And then, Dr. LaHaye pointed out there is the *committed Christian,* who is dedicated, with strong moral values, is concerned about the moral breakdown around him, usually votes for those who share his moral values, and opposes practices that violate biblical standards.

Dr. LaHaye clearly drew the lines of battle when he concluded, "The battle for the future of America will be fought between committed humanists on the one hand and committed Christians on the other."

By now you may be asking, " 'What do I do?' 'Should I get involved in the issues?' 'Should I speak out?' 'Is it too late to save our nation?' 'Do I have the 'right' to be heard?' "

The answers are: There is much that you can do. Yes, you should — and must — get personally involved in the fight. Yes, speak up and let your voice be heard. No, it is not too late to save our nation. Yes, you have the "right" to be heard — your opinion is valuable.

The first step is to evaluate your own beliefs and your personal relationship to God. Perhaps you have accepted the philosophy of humanism and believe there is no God and that you alone can save yourself. If so, before your relationship to God can be corrected, you must admit that you have sinned and stand in need of the Saviour, Jesus Christ.

Or you may be a Christian but have had your mind influenced by the doctrines of secular humanism, making it difficult for you to accept God's absolute moral laws as your guide to daily conduct. The question of sin is not to be treated lightly. Dr. Menninger, author of *Whatever Became of Sin?* described sin as ". . . a transgression of the law of God; disobedience of the divine will; moral failure."

He further described sin as man's "humanistic" attitude toward God. "Sin has a willful, defiant, or disloyal quality; someone is defied or offended or hurt."

You need not despair, however; your sins can be forgiven because Jesus Christ, God's Son, came to earth, lived a sinless life, died on the cross for our sins, was buried, rose from the dead, ascended into heaven and now sits at the right hand of God.

The Bible teaches us that when we trust in Christ as our Saviour we receive eternal life and are "born again" by the power of God. I urge you to accept Jesus Christ as your personal Saviour at this very moment, and then begin to pattern your daily life after that of Jesus Christ and live by God's absolute moral laws.

BECOME INFORMED

If you expect to be effective in your community, you must be informed on the issues. Your facts must be straight. My suggestion is that you read some books that cover the basics. These can be purchased at the bookstore or borrowed from your public library.

Be informed on political issues so that you can communicate the proper facts and information to your friends. (A starting point would be to pass this book on to a friend when you have finished reading it).

You will find that you are only one of a growing number of informed citizens who are no longer sitting on the sidelines but are "getting into the fight."

THE FUTURE IS BRIGHT

No, America is not a godless nation without moral values. The overwhelming majority of people in America are, at the least, moralists. The Gallup Poll revealed that 94 percent of our population is theistic in their beliefs and only 4 percent explicity deny the existence of a Supreme Being. George Gallup further revealed in 1976 that ther are 50-million Americans who claim to have born-again experience, and over 100-million people in America are church members. This includes Jews, Catholics, Protestants and others who take the Bible as the base for morality. There are another 30 to 50 million who were raised in a Christian environment and look to the Bible as the foundation for public and private morality. They may not be professing Christians, or even attend church, but they believe in biblical morality.

With such an overwhelming number who subscribe
to the Judeo-Christian moral system, why, then, are
we seeing our nation move toward secularism? It is
evident that the Christian community has been so
busy with its own affairs that we have allowed a
dedicated minority of humanists to infiltrate the institutions that are most effective in molding the minds of
the citizenry: the educational system, the media, entertainment, music, the arts, and the government. While
we sit idly by, approximately 50 million school-age
children are being systematically "programmed"
with the doctrine of humanism —right now!

But we can no longer refuse to get involved. We
have the overwhelming numbers on our side. It is time
for the sleeping giant to arise. There is power in numbers. Where one voice may be dim, a thousand — or a
million or 20 million — will be heard. There are many
pro-moral organizations across the nation. Find one.
Join it and contribute your time and your money to it.
And start with your church!

GET INVOLVED IN POLITICS

Webster defines politics as "the art or science of
government, of guiding or influencing governmental
policy, or of winning and holding control over government . . . competition between groups or individuals
for power and leadership."

Three-fourths of the people in the world live under
some form of totalitarianism, with their government
being controlled by a very few people. The uniqueness
of the American form of government rests in the fact
that every citizen may exercise political power at the

polls. Our guarantee of freedom of speech allows and encourages free and open debate of political issues.

Any group that feels its cause or belief will be affected by the enactment of certain laws may attempt to persuade the political machinery to move in its direction. Or if a group of citizens feels that the government is interfering in their lives where it should not, they have the right to take their cause to the American public to enlist as many people as they can in an effort to change the governmental involvement.

Christians and morally-minded citizens should not buy the myth that you must separate politics and religion. You cannot separate them. While we believe in separation of church and state, we still have the responsibility to influence our political system toward the traditional Judeo-Christian code of ethics. Each one of us has a certain amount of influence over others, and it is our responsibility to use that influence.

Professor Laurence Tribe of Harvard told the *New York Times.* "The tradition of the intermixture of religion and politics is too ingrained in our national life to be eliminated. It is extremely important to the principle of freedom of speech that this process not stop, just because some are distressed by the contents of the speech or the speaker."

In the September 15, 1981 issue of *Newsweek,* George F. Will said in an editorial, "Don't blame evangelicals for inflating abortion as a political issue. The Supreme Court did that by striking down fifty state laws which expressed community judgements about the issue. Those who oppose those judgments got them overturned by fiat, not democratic persuasion. There were 1.4 million abortions last year; and the forces that made that possible want subsidies for abortions, knowing that when you subsidize something you get more out of it. Yet we are told that it is the evangelicals who are aggressive about abortion. Evangelicals did not set out to alter social teaching through many measures that homosexual and heterosexual relations represent only different 'preferences,' or, as some call it, 'orientation among lifestyles.' Militant homosexuals are responsible for this and for making a hot political issue of government attempts to inculacate new attitudes."

MAINTAIN ACCESS
TO THE AIRWAYS

Freedom to preach the Gospel is a guarantee given by the Constitution of the United States and there must be no encroachment of government on this basic right.

Some say that the Gospel advances best in times of severe persecution and restriction, but the facts do not back this up. Admittedly, Christ's church will always survive even under the worst of conditions, as we have witnessed in Russia, China and other places. But even though the church survived, how many millions of souls in these countries were born, lived and died without once hearing the Name of Jesus Christ because of the suppression of the Gospel? The truth of the matter is that the Gospel flourishes best in a climate of free speech and movement. The millions of believers in the United States are the direct result of the freedom to preach the Gospel.

You don't have to be an expert in political science to predict what will happen when an anti-God government takes power in a country. The church is immediately refused access to the public airways. As a policy of the government, as evidenced by Russia, China, Cuba, Nicaragua and East Europe, the people are denied the freedom of preaching the gospel via the airways. Central America, as a whole, is on the verge of communist takeover; and when it happens the Gospel will be suppressed.

The countries that have succumbed to communism are clear evidence that a totalitarian government creates an anti-Christian ideological climate. The various means of communication and persuasion are used to indoctrinate people in the basics of the official ideology, while Christianity is attacked in both its doctrine and its practical application and is denied the means of defending itself. In such a climate, ideological barriers are established in the minds of the people, and they become closed to the Gospel.

SEPARATING THE STATE FROM GOD

In order to bring about a complete secularistic society, the voices of the opposition must be silenced or rendered ineffective. Of course the most powerful voice against secularism is the Church — more particularly, the evangelical churches.

The humanists face a dilemma: They cannot silence the voice of the church by law or force, for it is protected by the Constitution of the United States. But, they reason, there are other ways to attain the same net result. If you cannot silence the outcry of the church members by law, then you trick — or intimidate — them into "believing" that they do not have the "right" to speak out and be heard, and that "freedom of religion" is strictly confined to the practice of your own religion — within the four walls of the church building!

Have these tactics worked?

You had better believe they have!

Through various humanist organizations such as the American Civil Liberties Union and others, humanists have virtually paralyzed the American Christians in their attempt to speak out. This has been done through a calculated, studied, intentional, misinterpretation of the concept of separation of church and state. And they sit back and laugh at the stupid Christians for being so gullible.

The true intention of "separation of church and state" is, in fact, vital to our survival as a free people. Christians champion its true meaning. However, the Christian people have fallen into the trap of accepting the humanist interpretation to mean "separation of state and **religion.**" The humanists have convinced the Christian community that they are not to interject **morality** into politics or social issues.

The simple truth is that it is the **duty** and **responsibility** of the church to "speak out" on the morality of social and political issues. This is why the founding fathers formed our government in such a way that the church would be unhindered in its righteous influence on law, government, politics and society as a whole. They knew that the tendency of men was toward selfishness and evil, so the church was to be the great influence of righteousness on all areas of national life. This is why they placed the practice of religion on an equal basis with government. The church was not to be subservient to the state, so that it could — without fear — influence all of society with righteousness and morality. So, if the church **fails to speak out** on the issues of the day, it is failing in its duty to our society.

Separation of church and state is very simple. It becomes complicated only when you try to make the founding fathers say something that they didn't say. Let's let them speak for themselves. We don't need the humanist-twist to it for us to understand what they said.

Robert L. Cord, a professor of political science at Northeastern University in Boston, has said, "Certainly the framers of the Constitution and the Bill of Rights believed in the principle of Church-State separation and quickly added it to the organic law of the infant United States of America in 1791. However, those who authored and ratified that constitutional principle were not thereby mandating a complete **legal secularization of the American Republic;** far from it. In matters of faith, the founding fathers, and the American public they represented, are best described by U.S. Supreme Court Justice William O. Douglas's characterization of 1952: **'We are a religius people whose institutions presuppose a Supreme Being** . . .

"When the words and actions of the early Congresses and presidents of the United States are viewed in their proper historic context, it becomes clear that the First Amendment's Establishment clause was designed by its framers to prevent the establishment of a national religion or the placing of any one religious sect, denomination, or tradition into a preferred legal status which characterized religious establishments" (*National Review*, January, 1982) (emphasis added).

It is amazing how words can be twisted, taken out of context, or given a different meaning than the original intent, and then be used through the tactics of confusion and intimidation to paralyze those who disagree. Unfortunately, the Christian community has not taken the time to examine the truth in this matter and has simply accepted the humanist's fraudulent interpretation.

BECOME AN INTERCESSOR

In his book *War in the Spiritual Realm, the Ultimate Field of Battle*, Wyatt Lipscomb states, "There are sixteen officials directly over each of us in our form of government. The Key Sixteen over you are: The United States president (1), The Supreme Court justices (9), Your United States senators (2), Your congressman (1), Your governor (1), Your state senator (1), Your state representative (1).

"Each one of us has a responsibility to bring each one of these persons under the power of prayer. These are the people directly over each individual. When you pray for your own elected official, it influences the entire body. Each one of us has the responsibility to pray for those in authority over us (1 Tim. 2:1-2)."

In obedience to God's command to pray for those in authority over us, we should begin by knowing who they are and how they affect our daily lives. When you break your prayer-responsibility down to these "key sixteen," the task becomes manageable and you feel that you can be effective. The fact is, you pay their salaries, and what they do affects you and your family. So you have a personal interest in them and their actions.

THE BATTLE AHEAD: A WARNING

Here is a word of **warning!** In the near future there

will be brutal attacks on the churches and radio and television ministries, brought on by the ACLU and other humanist organizations. These attacks will be taken to the highest courts in the land. In fact, we are already witnessing the first blasts of a heavy barrage of propaganda against the conservative Christian leadership. The effectiveness of the Christian voices is causing great consternation in the humanist movement. It has been dealt a severe blow and is just now regrouping for a counter-offensive.

To the surprise of many, this attack is coming from both inside and outside the organized church, with large numbers of "liberal" clergymen as outspoken opponents of the pro-morality movement. However, we should remember that "liberal" theology is humanism in theological terms.

It sounds incredible, but pastors have been prosecuted and jailed, and — for the first time in America — at least one church has been padlocked for refusing to submit to government licensing and control. Pressure from governmental agencies has forced religious bodies to form interdenominational groups to study the situation and to devise plans to legally resist the government agencies' attempt to register, approve, disapprove, license, or control them. We must learn from the experience of other countries who are now living under a totalitarian system. The government of Rumania, for example, has a new "regulation" that says that any church buildings erected without government "approval" will be confiscated or demolished. In Czechoslovakia, a 65-year-old priest has been found guilty of "obstructing state supervision of the church." His "crimes" were **holding unauthorized services** and **producing religious literature.**

I have discussed these issues with many of the

Christian leaders in our nation today, and they believe, as I do, that if the trend is not reversed we will see the day — here in America — when the only "legal" church will be the one "registered" with the federal government. The government can then impose its "guidelines" on these churches, as is now being done in Russia and other communist countries. Pastors and church leaders should never submit to church "registration" with the government. To "register" is to submit to a higher authority.

Many in our society interpret "religious freedom" to mean that the government has granted religious freedom to the people as a "privilege."

It is not a privilege! **It is a RIGHT!**

Religious freedom is a right granted by the constitution of the United States. And the Christian community must steadily resist any abrogation of this right.

Well-known personalities are beginning to take to the airways to discredit the pro-morality movement in America. One of the notables is Norman Lear, a man who has made a fortune producing some of television's most immoral and offensive programs. He has vowed to fight the efforts of the people trying to bring decency back to television. He has organized a group called "People for the American Way." He states: "People for the American Way will head into the '80s seeking to help Americans maintain their belief in self; to reaffirm that in this society the individual still matters; that there is more reason to continue to believe in the future than to dispair of it; that to improve the quality of life we must strengthen the common cords that connect us as human beings and as citizens."

It is superfluous to say that Mr. Lear's interpretation of "belief in the future" sounds much like the humanist rhetoric we have heard so often before. Could he possibly be so deluded that he believes that the inane television fare he has piped into the American home helps to "improve the quality of life?"

Or, could it be that the pressure on sponsors and the networks to clean up television has made some of his productions unmarketable and is causing him to lose a fortune in profits?

A NEW DIRECTION

Be encouraged! There is a fresh breeze in the air! Our prayers and labors are beginning to affect this nation. There is no question that America is moving toward the greatest spiritual awakening in its history. All indications point in that direction. It is cause for rejoicing!

This was verified by the results of a recent survey conducted by Dr. John Pollock, a former professor at Rutgers University, on "American Values in the Eighties." Dr. Pollock said, "The increasing impact of religion on our social and political institutions may be only the beginning of a trend that could change the face of America. I never expect again as a social scientist to see anything as powerful in explaining so much of what Americans do. People are judging things in moral terms . . . *they are using religion privately and in the public sphere.*"

Those who believe in the moral principles upon which our nation was founded are speaking out and getting involved in the full spectrum of our nation's political life and thought. The informed, aware Christian citizen is saying that he will no longer stand in silence and watch the disintegration of the family, the brainwashing of our children in the public schools, the spread of pornography, approval of deviant life-styles, growing crime in the streets, rebellion in the schools, corruption in government, and the deterioration of America as a strong, powerful nation.

Gradually, those in politics, academia, the media, and the decision-making positions are taking this moral movement seriously.

I firmly believe that **God's hand is still on America** because of the millions of born-again believers here. Without them this nation would have been destroyed long ago. I do not believe that God will forsake America, because it is His principal instrument in getting the Gospel out to the other nations of the world. As long as America has this righteous, praying, giving, army of believers, He will continue to bless and protect it.

I believe that America is on the verge of a great awakening among His people to the real threat — **the lie** — secular humanism. The Christians are beginning to understand the strategy of Satan and how humanism has affected the thinking and life-styles even of the believers. Understanding this "world system," they will cast it off and turn to God in repentance, bringing about the greatest spiritual awakening this nation has ever witnessed.

I also foresee extremely rough times ahead, even to the point of some of God's ministers being arrested, prosecuted, and jailed for their refusal to submit to anti-God federal regulations designed to hinder the work of the church. Also, I believe the full weight of humanistic pressure will come against the thriving Christian school movement. The proliferation of Christian schools is a threat to the humanistic dream of ridding the world of the concept of God, and they will not stand idly by and allow it to continue to grow. They will attack it — unmercifully!

Even with the threat of reprisals, we must continue to *speak out* on the vital issues of the day — *to inform, challenge, enlighten, educate, encourage, expose* and *minister* His Word with love and compassion.

I am convinced that the decade of the eighties could well be the "decade of the Church." We have a great mission and responsibility to our generation of people.

I believe there will arise in this nation a large number of talented, moralistically sound, lucid, and courageous men and women who will enter the political arena — with all its heat and controversy — to take the leadership of this nation and guide it back into the mainstream of moral, financial, and political sanity.

The most important people in bringing about a spiritual renewal in this nation could very well be those elected officials who will fill the offices in our state capitols, the House of Representatives, and the Senate of the United States.

While our ministers and spiritual leaders can "call for action," those elected officials can **act!**

We can turn a nation back to God.

An opportunity like this may never come again!

MORE FAITH-BUILDING BOOKS
BY HUNTINGTON HOUSE

GLOBALISM: AMERICA'S DEMISE, By William Bowen, Jr., $8.95 (hard back). The Globalists — some of the most powerful people on earth — have plans to totally eliminate God, the family and the United States as we know it today.

Globalism is the vehicle the humanists are using to implement their secular humanistic philosophy to bring about their one-world government.

This book clearly alerts Christians to what the Globalists have planned for them.

MURDERED HEIRESS ... LIVING WITNESS, by Dr. Petti Wagner, $5.95. This is the book of the year about Dr. Petti Wagner — heiress to a large fortune — who was kidnapped and murdered for her wealth, yet through a miracle of God lives today.

Dr. Wagner did indeed endure a horrible death experience, but through God's mercy, she had her life given back to her to serve Jesus and help suffering humanity.

Some of the events recorded in the book are terrifying. But the purpose is not to detail a violent murder conspiracy but to magnify the glorious intervention of God.

THE HIDDEN DANGERS OF THE RAINBOW: The New Age Movement and Our Coming Age of Barbarism, by Constance Cumbey, $5.95. A national best-seller, this book exposes the New Age Movement which is made up of tens of thousands of organizations throughout the world. The movement's goal is to set up a one-world order under the leadership of a false christ.

Mrs. Cumbey is a trial lawyer from Detroit, Mich., and has spent years exposing the New Age Movement and the false christ.

TRAINING FOR TRIUMPH: A Handbook for Mothers and Fathers, by Dr. W. George Selig and Deborah D. Cole,

$4.95. Being a good mother and father is one of life's great challenges. However, most parents undertake that challenge with little or no preparation, according to Dr. Selig, a professor at CBN University. He says that often, after a child's early years are past, parents sigh: "Where did we go wrong?"

Dr. Selig, who has 20 years of experience in the field of education, carefully explains how to be good mothers and fathers and how to apply good principles and teachings while children are still young.

Feel Better and Live Longer Through: THE DIVINE CONNECTION, by Dr. Donald Whitaker, $4.95. This is a Christian's guide to life extension. Dr. Whitaker of Longview, Texas, says you really can feel better and live longer by following biblical principles set forth in the Word of God.

THE DIVINE CONNECTION shows you how to experience divine health, a happier life, relief from stress, a better appearance, a healthier outlook, a zest for living and a sound emotional life. And much, much more.

THE AGONY OF DECEPTION by Ron Rigsbee with Dorothy Bakker, $6.95. Ron Rigsbee was a man who through surgery became a woman and now through the grace of God is a man again. This book — written very tastefully — is the story of God's wonderful grace and His miraculous deliverance of a disoriented young man. It offers hope for millions of others trapped in the agony of deception.

THE DAY THEY PADLOCKED THE CHURCH, by E. Edward Roe, $3.50. The warm yet heartbreaking story of Pastor Everett Sileven, a Nebraska Baptist pastor, who was jailed and his church padlocked because he refused to bow to Caesar. It is also the story of 1,000 Christians who stood with Pastor Sileven, in defying Nebraska tyranny in America's crisis of freedom.

BACKWARD MASKING UNMASKED Backward Satanic Messages of Rock and Roll Exposed, by Jacob Aranza,

$4.95.

Are rock and roll stars using the technique of backward masking to implant their own religious and moral values into the minds of young people? Are these messages satanic, drug-related and filled with sexual immorality? Jacob Aranza answers these and other questions.

SCOPES II/THE GREAT DEBATE, by Louisiana State Senator Bill Keith, $4.95.

Senator Keith's book strikes a mortal blow at evolution which is the cornerstone of the religion of secular humanism. He explains what parents and others can do to assure that creation science receives equal time in the school classrooms, where Christian children's faith is being destroyed.

WHY J.R.? A Psychiatrist Discusses the Villain of Dallas, by Dr. Lew Ryder, $4.95.

An eminent psychiatrist explains how the anti-Christian religion of Secular Humanism has taken over television programming and what Christians can do to fight back.

YES, send me the following books:

_____ copy (copies) of **Globalism: America's Demise** @ $8.95   = _____

_____ copy (copies) of **Murdered Heiress . . . Living Witness** @ $5.95   = _____

_____ copy (copies) of **The Hidden Dangers of the Rainbow** @ $5.95   = _____

_____ copy (copies) of **The Divine Connection** @ $4.95   = _____

_____ copy (copies) of **The Agony of Deception** @ $6.95   = _____

_____ copy (copies) of **Training for Triumph** @ $4.95   = _____

_____ copy (copies) of **The Day They Padlocked The Church** @ $3.50   = _____

_____ copy (copies) of **Backward Masking Unmasked** @ $4.95   = _____

_____ copy (copies) of **Scopes II/The Great Debate** @ $4.95   = _____

_____ copy (copies) of **Why J.R.?** @ $4.95   = _____

_____ copy (copies) of **A Reasonable Reason To Wait** @ $4.95   = _____

Enclosed is: $ _____ including postage (please include $1 per book for postage) for

_____ books.

Name _____

Address _____

City and State _____ Zip _____

Mail to Huntington House, Inc., P. O. Box 78205, Shreveport, Louisiana 71137

Telephone Orders: (TOLL FREE) 1-800-572-8213, or in Louisiana (318) 222-1350